Writers' & Artists' G

How to Writ

ABOUT THE AUTHOR

William Ryan is the author of five novels, including the *Captain Korolev* series. His work has been shortlisted for numerous awards, including the Theakston's Old Peculier Crime Novel of the Year, The Kerry Group Irish Fiction Award, the HWA Gold Crown for Historical Fiction, the Crime Writers Association's Steel, Historical and New Blood Daggers and the Irish Crime Novel of the Year (four times). His next novel is *The Winter Guest* (Bonnier Zaffre, 2022). William teaches creative writing at City University in London having previously taught at the University of East Anglia and is the lead tutor on the Writers & Artists 'Fiction Writing' courses.

To find out more about writing courses offered by Writers & Artists, including 'Fiction Writing: Fundamentals' and 'Fiction Writing: Advanced' which are taught by William Ryan, go to www.writersandartists.co.uk/events-and-courses

'Taking Bill's course was one of the best decisions I've made as a writer. His classes combined useful lessons on crafting a novel in all its component parts, and offered a close reading of each writers's text. His insightful critique of my prose cut to the heart of what did and did not work, and his kind encouragement left me motivated to keep pushing myself to grow as a writer. And all of this while creating a warm and welcoming atmosphere in which students felt confident about sharing their work. Worth every penny.'

Tammye Huf
author of *A More Perfect Union* (Myriad 2021)

'I've been lucky enough to attend several workshops run by Bill, and can't recommend them enough. They really opened my eyes about what it takes to turn a good idea into the finished article, teaching me about plot structure, character development, and how to really make a scene come alive. My debut novel [published] in April 2018, and I'd credit Bill's workshops with helping me get this far.'

Robert Scragg
author of *What Falls Between the Cracks* (Allison & Busby 2018)

Writers' & Artists' Guide to

How to Write

HOW TO PLAN, STRUCTURE AND WRITE YOUR NOVEL

William Ryan

B L O O M S B U R Y   Y E A R B O O K S
LONDON • OXFORD • NEW YORK • NEW DELHI • SYDNEY

BLOOMSBURY YEARBOOKS
Bloomsbury Publishing Plc
50 Bedford Square, London, WC1B 3DP, UK
29 Earlsfort Terrace, Dublin 2, Ireland

BLOOMSBURY, BLOOMSBURY YEARBOOKS, WRITERS' & ARTISTS'
and the Diana logo are trademarks of Bloomsbury Publishing Plc

First published in Great Britain 2021

A catalogue record for this book is available from the British Library

ISBN: PB: 978-1-4729-7874-5; eBook: 978-1-4729-7875-2

2 4 6 8 10 9 7 5 3 1

Typeset by Deanta Global Publishing Services, Chennai, India
Printed and bound in Great Britain by CPI (Group) UK Ltd, Croydon CR0 4YY

To find out more about our authors and books, visit www.bloomsbury.com
and sign up for our newsletters

CONTENTS

INTRODUCTION vii

CHAPTER 1

Getting started 1

Organising your time and space 1 | Formatting, saving and revising 5
Networking, learning and staying well 9 | Summary 11

CHAPTER 2

The basics 15

Why *this* novel? 15 | Point of view 18 | Single POV or multiple POVs? 19
First-person POV or third-person POV? Or all-seeing narration? 21
POV rules (or rather, guidelines) 25 | Tense 27 | Some general points 29 | Summary 35

CHAPTER 3

Research, atmosphere and setting 37

What should you research? 38 | Handling research 53 | Summary 56

CHAPTER 4

Central characters 61

Building a central character 63 | Revealing the central character 81
Can your central character carry the novel? 84 | Have you chosen the right central character? 86 | Summary 87

CHAPTER 5

Subsidiary characters 89

Why do you need *this* particular subsidiary character in your novel? 89
Who are they? 94 | Managing characters 104 | Summary 107

CHAPTER 6

Plot 109

Dramatic world 110 | Three-act structure 114 | First chapters and prologues 115 | Act one: the beginning 119 | Act two: the middle 126
Act three: the end 136 | Summary 140

CHAPTER 7

Writing scenes 143

Chapters and scenes 143 | Purpose 145 | Where should I start my scene? 150 | Who is telling the scene? 151 | How should you start? 155
Conflict, risk, obstacles and subtext 156 | Who is in control of the scene? 162 | When to end a scene 164 | How to end a scene 164
Summary 167

CHAPTER 8

Dialogue 169

The purpose of dialogue 169 | Control 173 | Motivation 177
Compromise 180 | Carrying dialogue 184 | Summary 188

CHAPTER 9

You've finished your novel – what do you do now? 191

Is it really finished? 191 | Identifying which agents to submit to 193
How to submit to an agent 198 | Why do you need an agent and what do they do? 210 | Negotiating a book deal 214 | Managing your relationship with your publishers 216
What do agents charge? 218 | Summary 220

RESOURCES 223
EXAMPLE SYNOPSIS 225 | SOFTWARE FOR WRITERS 228
INDEX 235

Introduction

Every writer is different, as is every story, and this makes constructing a universal guide to writing a novel a difficult task. Each writer, including you, will have their own approach to writing their novel, based on their personal preferences. There are very few firm rules that *must* be followed, or at least no rules that can't be broken or bent (often to good effect). With this in mind this guide doesn't attempt to tell you how to write your novel in a prescriptive way. Instead it offers you practical, step-by-step assistance with thc task in front of you and encourages you to explore the infinite number of options that are available to you. It will hold your hand, in other words, but allow you to make the important decisions for yourself – based on the needs of your novel and your own ambition.

To this end, this guide describes the central aspects of novel writing. Each chapter starts with a general overview of the area of focus followed by specific routes to explore and questions to ask yourself to identify your objectives and develop your approach. Hopefully, as a result, this guide provides a frame on which to assemble the various elements of your novel, as well as suggesting ways in which the story can be written.

In each chapter, I also give examples that illustrate the matter being discussed. I have used hypothetical novels of my own devising for this, rather than the more common method of referring to published novels. This approach has the advantage of flexibility; a hypothetical novel can be altered to explain multiple approaches to novel-writing tasks, while also demonstrating how decision making has a logical momentum of its own that can produce a more rounded story.

One of the primary aims of this guide is to encourage you to interrogate the creative decisions you make while working, and to challange the story that you want to tell. This means that the guide includes a lot of general questions, which you should be able to easily apply to your work in progress. The more questions you ask yourself, the more you will find out about your characters, and about your story, and about how you should approach it. It may seem that I am throwing a lot of the decision making with regard to your story right back at you – and I am. My purpose is not to tell you how to write your novel – it's to give you the tools to write it in a better way. By encouraging you to ask the right questions, I want you to make the right decisions based on how you, the writer, want to shape your story.

This guide is designed so that it can either be read in one sitting, from beginning to end, or be used as a resource that you can access as and when the need arises. If, for example, you have a subsidiary character that isn't working as well as they might, then rereading the chapter on subsidiary characters may provide a way forward. Sometimes, however, elements of novel writing appear in more than one place. For example, it would have been impossible to write the chapter on the structuring of a novel without talking about the role of a central character in the narrative. It is equally the case that a separate chapter devoted to central characters and their other functions within the novel is essential. I've tried to minimise repetition, but there are inevitable overlaps.

Last, but not least, writing a novel, like any substantial creative endeavour, involves hard work and discipline but this doesn't mean it shouldn't be an experience that gives you pleasure. In a sense, you are not only the writer of your novel, but also its first and most important reader, so remember to give yourself the pleasure of writing a novel that you really want to read.

CHAPTER I

Getting started

To complete a novel successfully, you will probably need to approach it as a long-term project. It's important to accept that it will soak up a significant part of your time and energy for a lengthy period. With this in mind, organising in advance is sensible and there are a few things you can do to make life easier for yourself.

Organise your time

Writing novels is a bit like running a marathon and, leaving aside the craft of writing, you finish a novel by putting one word after another until there are no more words to write. You can sprint from time to time, but you are more likely to get to the end by writing regularly and maintaining momentum. Therefore, it is a good idea to designate a period of time that you can devote to writing on a fairly frequent basis. If you start with a schedule that is achievable rather than overly ambitious, there's a better chance you'll keep to it and, therefore, that you'll make continuous progress. Even an hour three mornings a week, if used productively, will result in real results quite quickly. If you are able to add an afternoon every other weekend as well, so much the better.

Don't limit yourself to the schedule, however. Once you get into the rhythm of regular writing, keep an eye out for available time that you can take advantage of. If you're watching something on television that you're not really enjoying, then stop – the time you save may well be the perfect opportunity to get a few hundred words down.

Set yourself targets and track your progress

Another way to keep piling up those words is to set yourself targets. Any weekly schedule you construct for yourself is bound to be subject to interruptions from your work and personal life, but that shouldn't mean you're off the hook. If you set yourself a target of writing for five hours each week then – even if your schedule has to be adjusted – having a weekly target will encourage you to catch up on missed slots.

Similarly, when you sit down to write, set yourself a word count target for the session. Every word processing package has a word count facility which will tell you how much you have written. If you have an hour to write, that should allow you enough time to write 500 words if you're focussed, so put a little bit of pressure on yourself to hit that target. You can also set word count targets for the week, month or even year. If you keep track of what you achieve each week, you'll get a sense of progress, be able to compare your productivity from week to week and perhaps even see a general upward trend. Having an unusually productive week can be a real boost.

Finally, consider setting yourself a target date for completion of the novel. You can always adjust the target date if your progress turns out to be slower or faster than you expected, but having that endpoint in mind will help focus your efforts.

Find a place to write

The truth is you can (and should) write anywhere the opportunity arises – some of my most productive writing hours have been on busy trains. That said, at the beginning of this novel-writing process you're trying to build up a pattern of behaviour. If you are able to find yourself a space which can be yours alone for the periods you have scheduled for writing, that will help create that pattern. If that space is at home, try to make sure you have a desk or a table that is at a good height and a chair that supports your back, as well as adequate lighting. Make it, in other words, an environment that will be conducive to writing productively.

If the space is outside of your home you may have less control of your environment, but there may be other advantages in that homes often contain distractions that you can't ignore. I often write in libraries, but I know writers who go into their workplaces at the weekend when no one else is around, frequent coffee houses and even pubs – and I've already mentioned trains. In fact, if you have a regular commute it might be the perfect time to get some writing done, although possibly not if you're driving or cycling.

Find something to write with

I have a writing laptop that I use for nothing other than writing. It has most of any research I've done, organised so as to be easily accessible, including hundreds of photographs that I think may be useful to recreate, in my mind, the historical period I'm writing about. It also has all of the daily drafts of the project I'm working on so that if I change something and it doesn't quite work out as I'd hoped, I can go back and access the earlier version I was happier with.

The laptop is my preferred writing implement, but I also sometimes use my phone. I have a small phone stand and a fold-out keyboard that is a little wider than pack of cards, but thinner. The phone, the stand and the keyboard can comfortably fit into a jacket pocket and it enables me to make good use of what might otherwise be dead time when travelling or perhaps waiting around. It also has the advantage of being compatible with my laptop, as I can email my work to myself and cut and paste it. In the same way, I sometimes use shared PCs in libraries or other public places. Very occasionally I also use pen and paper, although this is a last resort for the simple reason that I will have to type it up later on. I also know writers who dictate their first drafts and have a software program that transcribes it into a word document.

How you write, and what you write on, is up to you but I'd encourage you to be flexible – particularly where different devices may allow you to be productive in situations that might otherwise not be.

Minimise distractions

If you plan to write at home, and you share your home with family or friends, discuss your writing schedule with them and try to get their support, particularly if they may be around when you hope to be productive. If they know not to disturb you for the hour a day you have set aside, it's probably going to be better for everyone. Be reasonable, however. If you plan to write in the kitchen, accept that other people may need to access the room from time to time.

If you are writing outside of the house and there are other people around, consider investing in a pair of noise reduction headphones or even just a pair of ear plugs. Many writers also listen to music to block out background noise.

As you probably know already, the biggest distraction you are likely to face as a writer is the internet, and all the wonderful information and diversions it contains. Whilst it is an invaluable resource for research, it can be a real danger to productivity. If you are writing on a laptop, tablet or phone, try using an internet blocker for the period you want to focus on your writing. I use one called *Freedom*, but there are others available. When I'm writing in a library, or outside the house I often carry an old phone without internet access, or if I have to have a smart phone for some reason, I use an internet and app blocker on that as well. I have a particularly productive writer friend who has no Wi-Fi in his home and doesn't own a smartphone. He accesses his email twice a day in the local library and reasons that anyone who really needs to get in contact with him will probably know his home phone number. I am a little bit jealous.

Format your novel correctly

If you're using a computer or tablet to write your novel, be sure to use the publishing industry's standard format. This isn't essential but when you send your novel to an agent or publisher, it will make your work look professional. In terms of font either 12pt Times New Roman or 12pt Courier New is probably best. You should have double spacing between each line and indent the first line of each paragraph, except for the first paragraph in a chapter or scene. If you have a change of scene or location in the middle of a chapter, it's a good idea to indicate this by leaving a two-line break.

Finally, don't number your chapters until you have finished your draft. The likelihood is they will move around during the course of writing and this will avoid having to re-number them all each time.

Quantity often leads to quality

Although it is nice to write the perfect sentence, sometimes you need to keep moving forward if you're going to complete your novel. I would always rather write 1,000 not very good words over the course of a day than 100 perfect words. It's not that I don't care about quality – I absolutely do – but I also know that those 1,000 words can be edited until they become perfect whereas a blank page cannot be edited into anything other than a blank page. First drafts are meant to be unsatisfactory but if you have a finished first draft, despite its weaknesses, you probably have the basis for a completed novel.

Rewrite as you go along

I always begin each writing session by rewriting what I've written during the previous session. This follows on neatly from the last point and is a good reason why you shouldn't worry too much about your first attempt at a passage or chapter. Aside from wanting to constantly improve the quality of what I've written, I also sometimes find it difficult to start writing when faced with a blank piece of paper so reading and rewriting the previous day's work reminds me where I am in the story as well as getting my writing brain warmed up to produce new material. It also improves, often considerably, the material I have written the day before.

Aside from daily rewrites, I also stop every 10,000 words or so and read over the novel up to that point to check that it reads consistently and that the story is moving forward in the way I want it to. This generally also involves a certain amount of rewriting but it does mean that the novel grows in an organic way, which I think is helpful. By the time I submit my final draft to my editor, most passages in my novels will have been rewritten multiple times and hopefully this results in the novel being solid structurally and the prose fairly polished. Whichever approach you take, there will be a lot of rewriting at some stage. Novels are only really finished when they cannot be improved by further rewriting by you or further editing by your editor or agent.

Keep a cuts file

One aspect of rewriting that can be very difficult is letting go of material that you have spent a lot of time and effort working on. While that material has to be removed, it doesn't have to be deleted in its entirety. I strongly suggest keeping a cuts file into which you can move paragraphs and scenes that don't seem to have a place in your story at that moment in time. If your opinion changes later on you can easily move them back into the main draft, so it makes removing them in the first place much easier. I have one for every novel I write and sometimes it can contain nearly as many words as the final draft.

Always protect your work

I tell students to remember to back up their work the whole time, and yet I have just had an unfortunate accident with a chapter of this very book, in which I lost several days' work I had only saved to a memory stick because of technical failure. The experience is still pretty raw so learn from my mistake and always, always, ALWAYS back up your work in at least two ways. I should have saved it on the laptop I was using, then saved it to the memory stick and finally sent a copy to myself on email. That way I would have had three different ways of recovering it if something went wrong. If your computer or tablet backs up to the cloud, which it probably should, it will be continually saving your work so that even if the laptop self-destructs you will have lost a minimal amount of work. However, don't rely on cloud backups alone – there are occasional glitches and it's best to be extra cautious. Nearly every writer has a story about losing work to some kind of back-up failure and I can only encourage you not to join our ranks.

If you write longhand, and some writers find this is the only way they can write, you may have a problem if the dog decides your notebook is too tempting, or if it is inadvertently lost or destroyed. If you have a smartphone, consider photographing your new work after each session just in case.

Make use of technology

There are a number of software apps designed to help you organise and keep track of your novel and, although none of them will do the writing for you, anything that helps you to organise and structure your work should be embraced. *Scrivener* is a writing app which is widely used by professional writers and allows you to storyboard your plot, manage your characters, catalogue research and will also put your writing in the correct format. *Scrivener* does nothing that you can't do yourself using spreadsheets, Word documents or even just stickers and pieces of paper, but it does make life easier for you by bringing it all together and there is nothing wrong with that. You may also find productivity apps useful, particularly if you need to write a certain number of words in a short period of time. These apps generally work by encouraging you to write quickly and telling you off if you write too slowly. I occasionally use one called *Write or Die* where I am rewarded with a picture of a kitten if I hit my target and a scary spider if I slack off. Even though it sounds ridiculous, it does seem to work and once those words are on the page, they can be improved.

Most word processing packages will also have a spellchecker and a grammar-checking facility. Poor spelling and grammar can undermine even the best ideas and writing so make use of these tools. In the case of grammar, if it's been a while since you had to think about this in earnest, refresh your memory with a guide, online course or teaching app.

Keep a notebook for your story ideas

It isn't strictly necessary that you have a notebook to do this – you can write or even dictate notes on your smartphone or a laptop – but it is sensible to keep a record when inspiration strikes. I know this because I often find notes of useful ideas that I would not have remembered otherwise. Personally, I like to have a small notebook close to hand that is dedicated to a particular novel or other project in progress. I like to write my notes by hand, but there is no particular reason for this and I suspect it is mainly part of my own ritual for beginning a novel. It is also advisable to ensure that your notes are as detailed and clear as possible. I have occasionally found myself trying to decipher my own illegible handwriting or puzzling over a note that is opaque as to its original meaning.

Join a writers' group

Writing can be a lonely occupation but it doesn't have to be, and there are real benefits to joining forces with other people engaged in a similar endeavour. There are writers' groups all over the country and many libraries, bookshops and adult education establishments facilitate them. A little bit of research should allow you to find one locally and even if not, there are online alternatives. A good writers' group meets regularly and has active members who share their work with each other, read the shared work carefully and provide supportive feedback to each other on what they have read. This kind of considered and constructive feedback is essential to your development as a writer. As a developing writer, you want to know what works well and what works less well and you also want suggestions and advice from readers who may see flaws, strengths and opportunities in your writing that you have missed.

There is also a real advantage to you in reading other people's work from that same critical and objective viewpoint. In order to read someone else's work usefully, you have to be analytical and constructive. It's not enough to say you don't like a sentence, you have to be able to explain why and also how it may be *changed for the better.* That ability to look analytically and constructively at someone else's work, which you will probably develop very quickly, is easily transferrable to analysis of your own work.

A word of warning, however. Writing is an activity that relies to a large extent on having confidence in your own ability. It's therefore very important that if someone shares their work with you in a writing group environment, your feedback should be supportive and constructive without being overly and unnecessarily negative. A writing group has to be built on trust and if you don't believe that you and your fellow participants have each other's best interests at heart then you should probably find another one.

Enrol on a writing course

There are literally thousands of writing courses, ranging from those that last an hour and tell you to about something very specific, to postgraduate creative writing degrees that aim to help their students produce finished novels. See what's available locally: adult education centres, libraries, universities and writing organisations often offer writing courses and most literary festivals hold writing masterclasses alongside the main events. Arden, Literature Wales, the Irish Writers Centre, Creative England, Creative Scotland, the Open University, Writers & Artists (the publisher of this book) and a number of other writing organisations provide teaching for writers of all budgets and abilities, often with financial support for those in need of it.

Not only will you probably find yourself applying the feedback you are given to your own story – which can be a real boost – but you'll have the opportunity to meet other writers in a position similar to yours. It's a great opportunity to share information and make useful contacts.

Stay healthy

Sitting at a desk for long periods of time is not particularly good for you. As mentioned before, it's sensible to have a desk and chair that work for you physically but also, if you're using a laptop, to get a stand, a freestanding keyboard and a mouse. If your screen is at eye level, you are putting less pressure on your neck and if you are using a keyboard and a mouse, you are less likely to be doing damage to your shoulders and wrists.

It's also important to take regular exercise. I often start the day with a walk or a cycle to wherever I will be working, which gives me time to think about my plans for when I arrive. There is something about thinking while doing something repetitive such as walking, cycling or running, that helps me find occasional inspiration and, if nothing else, it's a nice way to start the day. Likewise, if you are in the middle of a long writing session, do get up from time to time and go for a quick walk around the block. Aside from being good to break up long periods of sitting, thinking about the scene you are working on while you walk may well suggest new and useful approaches to take when you get back to work.

Summary

TIME MANAGEMENT AND TARGETS

- Devote a specific period of time to writing as often as you can.
  - If you're writing at home, make sure your family or housemates know your schedule.
- Set yourself targets – sessional, weekly, monthly, and even annual – for both writing time and word count.
- Give yourself a deadline. Set a target date for the completion of your novel based on your schedule and targets.
- To hit your deadlines and minimise distractions:
  - Invest in noise-reduction headphones or simple ear plugs to lessen background noise.
  - If it helps, listen to music.
  - Install an internet blocker app on all internet-enabled devices.

FIND A PLACE TO WRITE

- Write anywhere and everywhere.
  - Be flexible and write when the opportunity presents itself (e.g. on the train, or while you are waiting for an appointment).
- Try and find a well-lit space for yourself with a suitable desk or table and chair.

- If you're using a laptop, get a stand so that the screen is at eye level, and use a separate keyboard and a mouse.
- Take regular breaks away from your desk.

WRITING PRACTICE

- Use the publishing industry's standard format right from the very start.
  - A serif font (usually Times New Roman, 12pt) is easy to read and work with: double-space your text.
  - Indent the first line, except for the first paragraph of a chapter, or after a line break (e.g. new scene).
- Quantity often leads to quality, so just get the words down and edit later.
- Rewrite as you go along.
  - Review and, if necessary, rewrite your work from the previous session as a way to 'warm up' before you write new material.
  - Review your work every 10,000 words.
- Keep a 'cuts' file. If you want to remove a paragraph, scene or even a chapter from your novel, remove it but don't ever delete it. Instead, save to a cuts file or folder for future use: you never know when it might come in handy.
- Look after your work.
  - Save your work continually throughout a writing session.
  - Back up your work in at least three different ways (e.g. laptop, emails and external drive).
  - Make use of the cloud or online storage systems such as DropBox or Google Drive.
  - Scan or take photos of any handwritten notes or text to create digital copies that you can find easily.

- Software apps can help with your writing, organisation, productivity and/or editing. See 'Software for writers' on pages 228–31 in Resources for more information.
- Use the word processor's in-built grammar and spellcheck tools to clean up the text as you go.
- Always keep a notebook (and a pen) to hand, ready for when inspiration strikes.
- Join a writers' group but treat other members (and their work) with respect.
- Consider enrolling on a writing course.

CHAPTER 2

The basics

There are some decisions that a writer makes – and things that they do – which are largely invisible to a reader, unless they are done poorly. Considering the fundamental parts of your novel such as narrating perspective (point of view), the tense and other general stylistic points in advance is always a good idea. The more thinking you do about your story, the better. That said, novels can't always be planned *completely*. You will have to account for the inexplicable, and often the unpredictable, consequences of characters interacting with one another on the page, meaning your ideas will need to change and adapt during the writing process. Often, characters won't behave in the ways you expected them to; sometimes they will do their best to change the story, or at least their part in it. On some occasions they will need to be brought back under control but on others the direction in which they take the story may well help you to write a better novel. Maintaining flexibility when it comes to the decisions you make when writing your novel – and being ready to reroute *if* you think it will lead to an improvement – is an essential factor in writing a great book. Be ready to experiment with your story, change it if needed and try new approaches to individual elements or even the whole story if necessary. While it is important to know where you're heading when you start a novel, you may find that the road you take to get there is very different than you anticipate. You may even arrive at a destination you had not imagined at the start.

Why *this* novel?

It's often useful if you know, at the outset, why you want to write this particular story rather than any of the others that you might have considered. After all, a novel is a large, time-consuming project that requires considerable commitment, so it's worth taking a moment to ask yourself why you are undertaking it. Perhaps you have simply decided that you want to write a novel and have found a story that appeals to you, which is probably a good place to start. Or it may be that you love novels of a certain kind and are writing the novel that you really want to read but that no one has written for you. That was certainly part of the reason I wrote my first novel, *The Holy Thief*. I liked historical fiction and crime fiction and thought that a police procedural about a Moscow police detective investigating a 1936 murder would appeal to me as a reader, as well as a writer. I also took the view that if I was enjoying reading it as I wrote, then other people would probably also enjoy it, and many people did.

There were, however, other reasons why I thought *The Holy Thief* would be a novel that would have interesting elements aside from the main narrative. At their core, detective novels are about truth and justice, both of which were very flexible concepts in Moscow in 1936. Detective novels are also about good and evil and things that we might now consider to be 'good' – concepts like personal morality, standing up for your beliefs and so on – were often considered 'evil' in the USSR. Meanwhile the execution, imprisonment and deliberate starvation of millions of innocent citizens, which we would consider evil, was approved of on purely political grounds. As a result, my detective's efforts to uncover the truth about a murder with political ramifications, and then to find a way to administer some kind of justice, would face many obstacles and present him with some interesting moral questions. In my novels, I often want to place ordinary people in extraordinary situations and see how they cope, so an ordinary detective working at the height of the Great Terror promised to be interesting for me to write (and read).

Alternatively, you might choose the novel you intend to write because an element of the story has a particular emotional significance for you. If that is the case, this is probably going to be a useful motivation when it comes to writing, and its emotional significance will probably translate into something similar for the reader. If you care about the story, they probably will too. However, it will be worth considering in advance how that emotional connection can best be reflected in your story – and whether you want the emotional element to be visible. For example, your story may be based on a family member's real-life experience or perhaps on your relationship with a close relative. Sometimes the story's personal connection to you may be obvious – a friend of mine has just written a novel based on her grandparents' wartime experiences, for example – and I think she will be very open about that. In other situations, the emotional element of the story will be visible to you and perhaps no one else, while still creating the kind of depth of emotion for the reader that you are seeking to create. My third Russian detective novel, *The Twelfth Department*, is on one level about my relationship with my son, who was an infant when I was writing it, although I'm not sure that anyone reading the novel would know this is the case. I used the central character's feelings about his eleven-year-old son to express some of my own thoughts about being a father, which was then still a very recent development. The addition of this element came quite late, however, as I had written most of the novel before I added in the father–son relationship. It was when I realised that the novel lacked the kind of depth and emotional significance I was looking for that I began to consider ways in which to achieve that, and remembered my detective had a son who I could usefully add in to the mix.

For most novelists there will be a particular theme or thought that they want to express or explore and your novel is probably no exception. It might be something about a place, or a person or a group of people about whom you have strong feelings, positive or negative. Your novel could be about a current topical issue or an historical one, or even about a philosophical idea. Once you decide on a theme or thought, you'll need to look at your story and consider how it might affect it for the better. If you were writing a romance novel and you wanted to use it to express thoughts on, for example, the polarisation of politics, then you would probably look at the couples' political leanings and make them different. If one character is liberal and the other character is conservative, then you immediately have a barrier to their romance, which will have to be overcome in some way. You could similarly bring in other characters, such as their friends and family, or have one of them running for political office, or both of them running for office, perhaps even against the other. While there could obviously be opportunities for comedy, that doesn't mean you might not have a serious point to make about tolerating differing opinions. It may well be by identifying a theme, as here, you bring the story itself into focus and allow it to shape the plot. We discuss plot in more detail in Chapter 6.

Not all novels have deep themes that are personal to their authors or weighty issues that they would like to address through the story, though. Indeed, many authors consciously avoid anything of that nature in their work. But having a theme or connection to the story can often help the writer with the plot and other elements of the novel, as well as creating depth and emotion that engage the reader. If you know why you want to write your novel, you may also have an idea as to why your reader might want to engage with the story and thus how best to shape the story to assist that engagement.

Point of view

One of the first things you will need to decide about your novel is which character or characters are going tell your story. Most novels are told largely, if not solely, from the central character's perspective, as it is their story and using their point of view has clear advantages. There are exceptions. The *Sherlock Holmes* novels and short stories, for example, are told from Dr Watson's perspective, while some novels are told by an omniscient narrator, although this is less common in contemporary fiction than it might have been in the past. The likelihood is that you will want to tell your novel predominately from the perspective of the central character, although you may use other perspectives as the story requires them.

Telling a story from a particular character's point of view, or 'POV', can be something that new writers can find tricky. Although most writing rules are more guidelines than rules, the guidelines when it comes to POV are relatively fixed. It's probably useful to start by thinking of the POV as equivalent to the camera angle in a movie. In other words, the character you choose to 'tell' a scene is the camera through which your reader sees the scene. The character can give us a wide-angled view of the setting or can focus the reader's attention on matters of particular interest. The character can tell us where they and the other characters are placed within the scene, what the initial situation is, and can allow us to observe the events that will take place. Unlike a camera, of course, the POV character has opinions, feels emotions and gets involved in the story.

Most novels, even if they use multiple POVs, will rely on the central character as the main storytelling voice. If that character isn't very appealing, however, carrying the novel via their voice becomes more of a challenge. The plot may be brilliant, the writing superb, but the book won't work if the central character fails to connect with the reader. It is worth taking time to ensure that the central character's storytelling voice is interesting and engaging to the reader. A lot of that will come from their character, but humour, intelligence, charm and an original view of the word that chimes with the novel's themes and subject are all elements that will help. If you think of your central character as the star in the drama that is novel, do they have star quality? Is the reader going to look forward to their appearance on the page, or not?

Single POV or multiple POVs?

I wrote my first three novels almost entirely from the central character's POV (except for a couple of chapters here and there for foreshadowing) and there are lots of advantages to this approach. A solitary and focussed POV can help create a bond between the reader and the central character, where the reader experiences the events of the story alongside the central character. This works particularly well with psychological thrillers, ghost stories and horror which rely on the central character not being entirely certain what is happening but fearing the worst. Perhaps the best reason for telling the story from a single perspective, however, is that it is easier to manage than using several. In practice, however, and I say this having now written two novels with multiple perspectives, the slight additional complexity is balanced by considerable storytelling benefits.

One disadvantage of having only one POV is that your central character will have to hear about events that they aren't present at from other characters. Telling the central character (and the reader) about an important event through dialogue seldom works as well as the character being present and telling the event through their experience of it. Action, in particular, is often better told through the POV of a character involved directly, rather than through dialogue after the fact.

Having an alternate storytelling viewpoint to the central character is also useful when it comes to establishing the central character in the reader's mind. The most obvious advantage is when it comes to giving a physical description. When you tell a story solely through the central character's POV, you are often reliant on rather clumsy approaches for this, such as the central character's looking into a mirror or examining a photograph of themselves. If you use the POV of another character, you can describe the central character much more naturally. This alternate POV can give the reader fresh insights into the central character's personality. This works particularly well when the insights differ from the central character's own idea of themselves. If your central character, for example, perceives themselves as being profoundly ordinary, it will make the reader reconsider if the other characters see them in a very different way. It can often be an interesting and useful experiment to rewrite a scene so that you see the central character from a different POV, even if you plan to solely use that of the central character.

Multiple POVs can also give the reader more information than the central character has, which is very useful for creating tension. If, for example, the reader knows, through an alternate POV, that another character plans to do something unpleasant to the central character, then the reader will be anticipating how the central character will deal with the upcoming situation, which hopefully means that they will want to read on.

There are also storytelling advantages to using multiple POVs. Describing the same scene from two POVs, for example, can lead to two very different perceptions of the same event, which can create ambiguity and intrigue for the reader. Switching POV repeatedly can also speed the story up by avoiding procedural scenes where the central character is not doing very much. For example, if your central character has to travel from A to B, you can avoid the journey by inserting a scene where another character is doing something more interesting, and then pick up with your central character when they have arrived. Switching POVs can also help make the most of dramatic events in the novel by looking at them and their effects from different perspectives. Similarly, because the central character is limited as to what they can really know about another character, so is the reader. However, if you adopt that character's POV, then the reader will inevitably have insight into their motivations and thoughts.

There are advantages to both approaches and your decision as to which way you want to tell your story may involve a certain amount of trial and error.

First-person POV or third-person POV? Or all-seeing narration?

Having decided how many POVs you are going to use, you will now need to decide whether your POVs will tell the story in the first person ('I') or the third person ('he' or 'she') or if you are going to use an all-seeing narration, which is essentially your POV as the author, and is neutral as a storytelling perspective. If you decide on third-person or first-person POV for a particular character, it is best to stick to that

POV approach for the duration of the novel, rather than moving the character's narration, say, from first to third as this can be confusing.

It is possible, of course, to tell the story using the second-person POV (as in 'you pick up the knife. It is heavy, but the blade is sharp') but this is relatively unusual and probably best to be avoided when you are starting out.

FIRST-PERSON POV

With first-person POV, the character is talking directly to the reader, telling them: 'I did this' or 'I am doing this'. The great attraction of reading from inside a character's head is that the novel can feel much more immediate. In a way, the reader 'lives' the novel alongside the character. They experience everything that the character experiences, see everything that they see and hear everything that they hear. However, that doesn't mean that the reader believes everything that the character believes and, of course, they may have very different perceptions of the reality that the character experiences. You, as the writer, will give the character loyalties and antipathies that the reader may not share and a personality that the reader may be wary of. Depending on the character, it can also be the case that the reader may doubt the character's observational powers or reliability. If the character sees a friend acting in a suspicious way, they may excuse the behaviour whereas the reader may not.

Generally speaking, having more than one first-person POV in a novel needs to be handled carefully as it can confuse the reader and as the central character is the focus of the story, they are better suited to first-person POV than other narrating characters. That having been said, first-person narration is common for prologues, where the POV character is sometimes obscured and may not reappear until much later in the novel, if at all. In crime novels, for example, the prologue might be told from a murderer's point of view, or from a victim's. In both cases, there are advantages to using first person – either to feel the terror of the victim or to get an insight, often equally terrifying, into the killer's motivation and character. If you are going to use more than one first-person narrator in your novel, be sure to make it clear to the reader who is narrating at any particular time (it's common to start chapters with the narrator's name).

First-person POV often has a dialogue quality to the prose, and it's important to remember that the character's personality and situation will impose certain restrictions on your writing. If, for example, you are writing from the perspective of a six-year-old child, it may read oddly if you use adult language and complicated similes. The voice you use will have to match the character and will have to be maintained throughout the novel unless a change can be explained by aging or some other change in situation. If you think the limitations that come with a particular character may be too restrictive, it may be sensible to switch to a third-person narration where you have a little more flexibility and distance.

THIRD-PERSON POV

With third-person POV, where the narrating character is 'he' or 'she', you, the author, are telling the story rather than the character. This means you have more discretion as to how you approach the storytelling and are not restricted by the character's personality or voice. You may choose a POV that is very close to the central character, perhaps directly quoting internal thoughts, or you may choose a more distant, more observational POV. You may also slide from one to the other, with the more descriptive and informational passages being told from a more distant third-person POV and the more intimate or introspective scenes being told from a much closer POV.

As with a first-person POV, the close third-person POV can read very much like dialogue and, as with first person, that can limit the language that your character will use but, because you can distance the POV when needed, this is a problem that can be fairly easily overcome.

Third-person POVs are commonly used for minor characters who only take the narration focus for a limited time. Sometimes you need to use a minor POV like this so that the reader can experience action first hand, rather than hearing about it, or perhaps so that the reader can acquire information or knowledge ahead of the central character, which can increase tension and anticipation. Third-person POV also allows you to identify the narrating POV immediately and clearly. Rather than 'I looked down at the chaos and tried to make sense of it', which leaves you still having to identify the narrative POV for the reader, you can write 'Sarah looked down at the chaos...' and the identification is done.

OMNISCIENT NARRATION

Novels that use an omniscient or all-seeing narration to tell all of the story are relatively rare these days – Vikram Seth's *A Suitable Boy* is one example – but that doesn't mean that it doesn't have its uses, particularly as an alternate POV. Omniscient narration differs from the other storytelling perspectives we've discussed in that it isn't focussed on a particular character's perspective on the story, but instead observes the events of the story from a more distant and neutral position. Omniscient narration is much more common in non-fiction than fiction and that's probably because fiction often relies on emotional engagement, whereas non-fiction is more detached. The reader of a novel is much more likely to be engaged by the central character and the story if it is predominately told from their perspective (whether first person or third person) because the reader experiences the story alongside the central character.

Novels also rely on conflict between the characters to move the story forward and create key dramatic moments. If the conflict is observed through an omniscient narration, it is difficult to give the conflict the same weight and drama that you can achieve with first- or third-person narration, where the reader has access to the POV character's thoughts and can experience, through the POV character, the reactions and emotions of the other characters in the scene.

However, this observational quality of an all-seeing narration, that does not have the emotional stake in a scene of a POV narration, does have its uses. If you want to summarise the situation quickly and efficiently, then all-seeing narration can work well. For example, you could use it to give an overview of the key characters in the novel and their relationships at the beginning of a novel, as well as perhaps explaining a little about the social and political situation in which the novel is set. Similarly, all-seeing narration is useful to tie up loose ends at the end of a novel, when it can be used to tell the reader what happens to the characters after the plot of the novel ends.

POV rules (or rather, guidelines)

The problem with rules when it comes to writing is that authors break them and often to good effect. Having said that, there are some pretty firm guidelines when it comes to POV. The most important general requirement is that the reader knows which POV character is telling the story at any particular moment and that that POV narration is credible within the parameters of their point of view. With those two aims in mind, the following are some suggestions as to how to avoid making errors with POV narration:

- **Be aware of the limits of your POV character's perception.** Your POV character is limited to what they can personally see, hear, feel, smell and taste. If they can't see themselves in a scene, they can't describe themselves. Likewise, if it would be impossible for them to hear what a character is saying on the other side of a field, then they can't tell the reader what that character is saying. It also means your POV character can't be certain what another character is thinking or feeling (unless the other character tells them). However, the POV character can *guess* the other characters' emotional state and thoughts, based on what they see and hear and their knowledge of the individuals. As in real life, your POV character may well be able to deduce other people's thoughts and emotions through their physical reactions, appearance and gestures. For example: 'She touched his hand and the look he gave in response made it clear that he felt the same emotion.' To avoid confusion, clearly signal to the reader when you are shifting POV from one character to another. My personal approach is to start a new scene (signified by a double line break) or even a new chapter when I want to change the narrating POV. Nearly always, I tell the reader about the shift in the narrating POV in the first line of the new scene or chapter. For example: 'John opened the window, inhaling the smell of the sea. Below him, a fishing boat moved slowly across the harbour's calm water.' The reader knows immediately where John is and that he will be telling the scene that will follow.

A clear break is probably the simplest way to handle shifts in POV, but some authors have shifts in POV mid-scene, mid-paragraph and, very occasionally, mid-sentence. As long as you remember to ensure that the reader is never confused as to which character is telling the scene, you have considerable flexibility – but if you have any doubts, make sure your intentions are clear to the reader.

- **Is a new narrating character POV really necessary?** If you are telling your story from multiple POVs, be aware that having too many of them can be confusing for the reader. If you are adding a new POV narrator for a scene, it's worth considering whether one of the more established POV characters could tell the scene just as well. If there is no particular reason to shift to a new POV, it's probably best to avoid it.
- **Be aware that a POV character's personality and perception will impose limitations.** Obviously, if a character is very young, of low intelligence or has some other challenge, then there may be limitations to how they see the world and how they can tell their story. While you may be able to work around such restrictions, there may not be sufficient benefit to doing so. You should also consider whether your POV character's personality is suitable

for a storytelling role. For example, if the character has a very neutral personality, they may not engage with scenes as effectively as a character with a more active personality. If your character is capable of astute observation and comment and has wit and intelligence, then they will be much better placed to comment on a scene than a character with none of these attributes.

- **If you are using multiple POVs to tell your story, do so creatively.** For example, you can retell a scene from a new POV to give a very different perspective. Similarly, you can use different POV characters' perceptions of an event to make them more complex. For example, if you are writing a novel about the American Revolution, using the viewpoints of both a revolutionary and a loyalist member of the same family might give a much more rounded picture of the conflict.

Tense

Traditionally, the majority of novels were written in the past tense but, recently, novels written in the present tense have become more common. Some authors and critics have taken public positions favouring past tense over present tense, whereas other authors, often the ones telling their stories using present tense, have a very different view. There are some technical differences between the two tenses and certain types of novels may be better told in the present tense rather than the past (and vice versa), but I'm not certain that either approach is better or worse although, having said that, after five novels in the past tense, I am currently writing a novel in the present tense and enjoying it.

PAST TENSE

The advantage of past tense is that your narrating character is telling the reader about events that they have already experienced. This means that they know the novel's story and how it ends, which allows them to hint at and foreshadow events which come later in the novel. It also allows the narrating character to lead into scenes or chapters with knowledge of what is about to occur. For example, a POV character could end a scene with 'I decided I needed to visit the Spencer family's house immediately. Little did I know what I would find there when I arrived.' That might be a little out of context, but you can see how it encourages the reader to read on to discover what might be waiting for the POV character at the Spencer house. That's not to say that you can't foreshadow in present tense, but it has to be handled less directly. For example, the POV character might have a suspicion as to what might await them at the Spencer family's house.

The main advantage of past tense, in my opinion, is that you have more narrative distance to work with. The reader can still have an intimate and close relationship with the POV character but, as the author, you have a little bit of perspective which can allow you to shape the story, what the characters observe, and how they observe it in a slightly more controlled way than with present tense. You are telling the story with past tense, as opposed to living it moment to moment with present tense, and that is often a good thing.

PRESENT TENSE

The flip side of having that distance and perspective on the story, and telling it rather than living it, is that sometimes you may have a story that benefits from the immediacy and tension that comes from the present tense. Psychological thrillers, for example, are often told in the present tense (and first person) because it can add to the claustrophobic intimacy and fear that the novelist is trying to create. It can also add a feeling of pace to stories that feature lots of action and excitement, as well as engagement to slower, more emotional stories.

It is often the case, but by no means always, that a novel told in present tense is told solely from one perspective. This is because switching out of a POV character telling the story in present tense can risk breaking the intimate bond between the character and the reader. If you are experiencing a present-tense story through a particular character, shifting away can be disconcerting.

MIXING TENSES (AND POVs)

You do, of course, have the option of switching tense when you switch POV. For example, your novel could feature parallel storylines, one set in the present and told in the present tense, and the other set in the past and told in the past tense. Some novels might start and end with a present tense, contemporary introduction and summation from the perspective of a character looking back on the story told in the novel, whereas the rest of the novel may well be told in the past tense.

Some general points to be aware of

Writing a novel is a journey of discovery and for many authors the journey is often towards a style of writing that suits them and the novel they want to write. It is very difficult to give general guidance on this because every writer is trying to do something different and has a different perception, when it comes to their own prose, of what is good, and bad. However, there are some elements that are worth considering when it comes to writing your novel, and worth bearing in mind when it comes to editing it.

KEEP CONTROL OF DESCRIPTIONS

A lot of writing involves description and it's wise to think carefully about what you need to describe and how you choose to describe it. Ideally, you should consider why each sentence, paragraph and chapter needs to be in your story – as in whether it moves the story forward or helps it in some other way. If you know what you are trying to do with a passage of writing, whether long or short, then you probably know what is important and what is less important. Bearing this in mind, if you spend too long describing an element of your story that isn't particularly relevant then, even if the writing is beautiful, it may be getting in the way of the story. For example, if you are describing the exterior of a building in which a scene will take place, it is probably worth considering why. There may be plot reasons why you need to describe an escape route, for example, or you may want to tell the reader something about the building's occupants or their personality through a description of their home but, if you don't have a need to describe the exterior in detail, then you probably should either do it very briefly or not at all.

If, on the other hand, you have a good reason for describing something, then you need to decide how to go about it. The primary purpose of a description, from a storytelling perspective, is to give the reader information that they need. Ideally, you want to do this in an efficient way – in other words you probably want to focus on details that are essential to understanding the story. You may want to extend the description past the essentials, but it's worth identifying what has to be communicated and building the description around it. Once you've achieved an efficient, focussed description, then you can concentrate on giving it the added extras that will make it pleasurable, as well as useful, for the reader.

Don't, however, over-describe. Descriptions that go on too long, and have no plot or character purpose, can soon become tedious for the reader and slow the pace of your novel down. It is often sensible to give the reader enough information to shape the description you intend, then allow them to fill in the rest from their own imagination. For example, if you were describing the exterior of a Renaissance palazzo, you could describe it in great detail, or you could give a very brief sketch of the building and focus on one element, say the massive iron-bound doors or the twisting ivy, which may allow the reader to create an image of the exterior that is personal to them.

Writing well is often about communicating the ideas, images and events that you have in your mind into the reader's mind. Your descriptions should therefore be accurate and precise so that someone who is familiar with the image that you are communicating will recognise it, and those that are unfamiliar will have enough information to create the image that you intend. If the reader is uncertain or is second-guessing you, then they may not be engaging with your story in the way you want them to.

KEEP CONTROL OF YOUR WORDS AND SENTENCES

Novels are built from sentences that lead from one to the other, and the words that fill them. However, be careful not to push your words, and the sentences that contain them, past the point of meaning or comprehension. Where possible, favour those words that are accessible for the majority or readers. Rare or unusual vocabulary runs the risk of excluding a reader from the meaning of a sentence, or making reading hard work rather than the pleasure it should be.

You should also be careful about the meaning of each word you choose. If you find yourself resorting to a slightly unfamiliar word, it's always sensible to double-check its definition to make certain you are using it correctly. You should also be aware of alternate meanings of words or phrases. For example, 'the man shot down the street' could mean he ran down the street very quickly or that he fired a pistol down its length. Even if the context will probably explain the sentence's meaning, be careful to avoid even momentary confusion for the reader. A smooth read, without distraction, is always best.

Similarly, busy and over-complex sentences also run the risk of confusing the reader. Long sentences with multiple sub-clauses, particularly if they contain unusual words and strained similes and imagery, are best thought about carefully and read aloud to make sure they sound good and that their meaning is clear. Be particularly careful with frontal adverbials – the sub-clauses we sometimes place at the beginning of a sentence. 'Wearing a suit of armour, John walked into the room' works better as 'John walked into the room, wearing a suit of armour'. This is because the latter version tells us instantly that John is the subject of the sentence and, without this knowledge, the wearing of the suit of armour doesn't have immediate meaning. It may sound like a picky point, but repeated frontal adverbials with no clear subject can irritate the reader.

As a general rule, I think it's best to know what you want to say in a sentence and then say it simply and efficiently. The sound and rhythm of a sentence, and the image you create in the reader's mind, is the secret to good writing. Less, often, is more.

ADVERBS AND ADJECTIVES

Adverbs and adjectives exist for a reason and 'to run' has a different, more general, meaning than 'to run slowly'. That having been said, writers can sometimes get carried away with their use of both adverbs and adjectives. 'A tall, slim man' is fine but 'a tall, dark, slim and handsome man' is probably not. Some writers have advised against using adverbs altogether, but that's impractical. What is sensible advice is to be careful with repeated use – not every verb needs an adverb. For example, 'They spoke quietly as they walked slowly to the wall, where they stopped suddenly', is probably a little heavy-handed.

TAKE TIME WITH WHAT'S IMPORTANT

If you take a step back from your story (always a good idea), you should be able to identify the moments that move it forward or are otherwise significant. Each chapter in your novel (and each scene within it) will probably have such a moment, whether it's an observation or a revelation or something else useful for your story. If your chapter (or scene) doesn't have such a moment then you may want to ask yourself whether it should. Presuming, however, that you have identified a particularly important moment, perhaps one which changes the direction of your story, be sure that you give it space. For example, a scene in which your reader meets an important character for the first time probably shouldn't be rushed while introductions to lesser or walk-on characters can sometimes be skipped over. When you read over your writing, look at it from your audience's perspective: ask yourself what they need to understand or be informed about, and check that you have given them all the information they need.

LOGIC AND CREDIBILITY

Anything can happen in your novel – provided you do the groundwork to establish the possibility of its happening. If, for example, you want spaceships to land outside your central character's house half-way through the action, this will be accepted by the reader *if* you give them warning that something like this might happen. If your novel is called *Aliens from Outer Space*, that would probably be a good start, but you could also introduce unexplained bright lights in the sky and other mysterious happenings in the preceding chapters so that the reader will be prepared for an unusual event.

The same is true of characters. If you want a character to behave in a way that might not immediately make sense, give the reader some reason to accept the behaviour. If, for example, you want the chairwoman of a local Women's Institute to turn into an action hero, establish her familiarity with firearms or show her ability in a martial art. Where novels sometimes go awry is that they fail to explain strange events or behaviour, or don't explain these things sufficiently for them to be credible.

Something else to bear in mind is the logical effect of an event. If your central character is unpleasant to another character, that will probably mean that the other character will not like them. If a character pulls out a weapon in the midst of an argument, the other characters present will probably need to acknowledge this in some way. How they acknowledge it is up to you, but if there is no reaction the reader will be concerned. This applies to the smallest of events in your novel. If a character is unexpectedly unhappy, the reader will want to know why. If a character has a piece of good luck, it is likely to have an effect, positive or negative, on their relationships with the other characters. The reader may not expect the effects of an event that you decide on, but as long as you explain the effects adequately, they will accept them. Logically, however, they will expect there to be some subsequent effect to any significant development and if you think through the ramifications and adapt your story accordingly, it will make it stronger.

CONVEYING INFORMATION

Over the course of your novel you will have to give your reader a great deal of information about the characters, the setting and the story. It is nearly always best to convey this information through action or observation of emotions and events rather than 'telling' it through dialogue or prose. For example, it is quite common at the beginning of a novel to want to give an introduction to an important character. When the reader sees this character, let's call him John, for the first time, it is perfectly acceptable to describe John as 'tall, good looking and with an easy smile' because this is an observation of his outward appearance. When, however, it comes to John's personality, it is better to *show* that John is dishonest through his actions rather than to tell the reader this. Similarly, if John decides to defraud an elderly neighbour, it is better to have an event in the novel showing him doing this, rather than conveying his actions through dialogue between the characters or some other less dramatic means. In essence, if you want to tell the reader about an event in your story, a character, a relationship, the setting or any other aspect of your narrative, it's best, where possible, to flag that up through action or observation.

Summary

	Pro	Con
Single POV/ 1st person	• Creates a bond between the reader and the central character. • Allows the reader to experience the action alongside the central character. • Easier to manage when writing.	• Central character has only limited knowledge and will hear about important events from subsidiary characters. • Central character cannot describe themselves.
Multiple POV/ 3rd person	• Can provide additional commentary on the central character's personality and physical appearance. • Provide information to the reader that the central character is not privy to. This is helpful to build tension. • Reader has access to different characters' thoughts and motivations. • Provides a different perspective to important scenes.	• More characters for the writer to manage and develop. • Each POV will need a distinct and recognisable voice. • Less likely to establish a bond between the reader and the multiple POV characters.
Omniscient	• Not focussed on a particular perspective or character. • Distant and neutral position. • Can tie-up loose ends and summarise action quickly and succinctly.	• Lack of emotional engagement; it only presents the actions. • More suited to non-fiction as it is 'telling' more than 'showing'.

CHAPTER 3

Research, atmosphere and setting

Some writers do very little research, if any at all, and some – including me – possibly do too much. All of us, however, are trying to create a logical and credible world for our novel to take place in; one that, ideally, the reader doesn't question. Research is often key to achieving that aim. If your novel is set in a world which is entirely imagined, either because the action takes place in the future or some parallel version of our present or past, its construction may not require much research, except possibly a knowledge of how other writers have created similar worlds. Similarly, novels set in the everyday world in which you live, about which you know everything, generally require nothing more than your existing knowledge. Most other novels will require at least some research, not only to ensure accuracy and authenticity, but also because the process provides useful information and detail, not to mention plot ideas, for your novel. If you do your research early, it can help shape your plot in the early stages. If you do it after you have started writing, you may find that some, or even all, of your story will have to be rewritten.

A novel is, on some levels, a little like a conversation in which the writer does all the talking but relies on the reader listening to the writer's story (and continuing to turn the pages). Generally, as writers, we would like reading our novels to be a smooth flow from first page to last. If a reader says that they couldn't put your novel down, that is probably close to what you're aiming for. If the reader is distracted at any stage, you should ensure that the distraction comes from outside of the novel rather than a mistake you have made within it. In addition, you want to establish early on your authority as a storyteller. There are times when you pick up a book and you know from the first page that the writer is confident of their story and knows how to tell it. As a reader, you know you can relax and enjoy the ride. That feeling of trust is what you want to give your readers in turn. Research, amongst other things, will help you to achieve this. Every fact or detail you reveal in the novel, whether about people, places or anything else, needs to be credible within the fictional world you have created. If something causes the reader to doubt the authenticity of your fictional world in some other way, then you have probably pushed them out of that story flow and failed to retain their interest. Unfortunately, you may well, at the same time, have lost their trust in you as a storyteller. The danger is then that they will put down the book and not finish it.

What should you research?

If you are writing fantasy fiction or a novel that takes place in a wholly imagined setting, you may think you are off the hook. However, you can still use real locations and details as the basis for your creation. And if you're writing a novel set in an historical or contemporary location, you can research much, much more. The safest approach is probably to research what you can and to double-check anything that might be questioned by the reader or leave them uncertain.

PHYSICAL LOCATIONS

If you are writing a contemporary novel, you should always visit any location that you are writing about, if at all possible. Even if you feel as though you know the location well, it is worth examining it *as a writer*, with any scene and characters that you plan to place there in mind.

First, consider the surroundings and architecture in terms of the events and requirements of the scene, deciding how the scene will work from a practical perspective, as in who will be placed where and how the action will proceed. Will there be other people about and how will that affect what transpires? Remember what time of day and year you're setting a scene and work out how your chosen weather will affect the action. Then consider if there are interesting features that you can use to give a strong sense of place or atmosphere.

Next look at the location through the eyes of the characters who will appear in the scene. Every character will have their own personal perception of the location and may also have a different, existing relationship with the place. For example, if your characters have lived nearby since birth, they will see the location in a very different way to someone who is experiencing it for the first time. They will also notice different things and perhaps see danger, or security, where a stranger would not. For example, if someone has grown up in a socially disadvantaged area, they may feel comfortable revisiting it, whereas someone from a more privileged area visiting for the first time may not. The location may also hold memories for them, which will perhaps be significant to your story. Conversely, a character who is new to a place will see it with fresh eyes, which can be useful when it comes to describing it for the reader. They may also feel themselves unwelcome or treated as an outsider, which can also be useful for your story. Remember to use all your senses, too. There may be sounds and smells that are unique to the location. If they are useful to create a vivid setting in your novel, why not use them?

Think, also, about the place from the *reader's* point of view. What details will give them a clear image of the place and enable them to understand how the characters will move around it. If there are challenges that the space presents, even if they do not materialise, you may want to mention them to the reader. For example, a character in a thriller may view a seemingly abandoned building as the ideal place from which an enemy may launch an ambush.

If you were setting a scene in a café, as an example, where your central character is meeting another character, you might want to give a description of the exterior to tell the reader what kind of establishment it is and a little about the neighbourhood where it is situated. You would probably also mention any information the narrating POV character already has about the café that is significant to what will happen in the scene. If the narrating character doesn't know the place, you will also probably want to record their first impression ('it looked expensive'). You will also probably mention any important details from the general setting, such as approaching sirens, tables on the pavement that may hinder a swift exit or some loitering police officers, particularly if they will have a role later in the scene. As a writer, you will also be thinking about the atmosphere you want to create. If you want the scene to be tense and suspenseful, you might set it at night when the street is deserted. Atmospheric details – a church bell that rings the hour, a sheen of rain on the pavement that reflects the streetlights, the way the central character's footsteps echo on cobblestones – may help achieve the effect that you're looking for.

If the meeting is to be a romantic one, remember that the narrating character will probably have chosen the location with this in mind and you should probably look at the cafe with their eyes to decide why they chose it. Perhaps there is a quiet table underneath the awning that is ideal for just such an assignation. Or perhaps it has a particular significance for the lovers ('it was where we had our first date'). Look at the cafe again for anything that might help create that romantic atmosphere and allow yourself to add details that may be helpful, such as a friendly waiter who takes a paternal interest in the lovers or a breaking plate if the meeting is not going to go well.

When visiting a location you aren't familiar with and may not be able to revisit, I really recommend that you take photographs and make notes about anything that may be of use to you as these will make it easier to recreate the place later on. In particular, take note of street names, shops, buildings, landmarks and anything that identifies the location. If there is something unusual, like a large pink statue in the centre of a square, your character will probably want to mention it in passing.

If you are trying to recreate your location during a particular historical period, it is still a good idea to visit even though it may have changed a great deal. Focus on the buildings or elements from the period that are still standing and remember that even if the buildings have changed, the layout of a street, or the contours of a landscape, may not. And if your location is much changed or you want to recreate a non-specific location, then it might be worth looking for a place with the kind of architecture, buildings or other details you need elsewhere. For example, almost nothing of medieval London still exists but there are comparatively well-preserved medieval streets in Lincoln and York.

Aside from a physical visit, there are other ways to build up an accurate picture of a time and place. A map from around the same time is always useful, it will give contemporary street names and tell you if the street map has changed, as well as possibly giving other information about buildings or features that no longer exist. In addition, local libraries and museums will often have old photographs, paintings, sketches and prints that will reflect a place's previous physical appearance. Depending on the period in which your novel is set, you may also be able to find a travel guide for the location you're researching. Travel guides have existed, in one form or another, for hundreds of years. Baedeker guides have been published in English since the 1860s, for example, but there are much earlier examples going back to the fifteenth century. They will often describe the important buildings and sights that should be seen by a respectable visitor, as well as where they should eat, drink and stay. Less reputable guides, such as *Harris's List of Covent Garden Ladies* (published annually in London from 1757 to 1795) were intended for a less respectable clientele and had somewhat different sights and experiences in mind, but that doesn't mean they won't reveal details that might be very useful for your fictional version of the past.

Even if you are imagining a location from scratch, it's worth basing your creation on an actual place. The island off the Devon coast in my 2018 novel, *A House of Ghosts,* is completely invented, but does have some slight similarities to Burgh Island and Lundy Island respectively. For my novel, I wanted the island to be close enough to the mainland to be visible from shore, but far enough away to be inaccessible in a storm. I wanted there to be a big house on the island as well as a lighthouse, a farm, cliffs, a beach and a small harbour. I started by drawing a map which gave me a sense of scale and helped me place the buildings

I wanted in relation to each other. In order to recreate the buildings themselves, I found similar buildings elsewhere and adapted them to my purposes. The lighthouse is based on the Galley Head lighthouse in Ireland and the farmhouse's original is located in Kent, rather than Devon. The Tudor country house is an amalgam of several houses, to which I added a cellar and an ossuary from Italy. Again, I drew a plan of each floor of the house so that I had a clear idea of the layout and scale. I used photographs I took myself, as well as images I sourced from the internet for the interiors. The candelabra in the library, for example, was discovered in an online auction catalogue and adapted for my purposes. In short, although the island was put together by me, it was built from real elements from elsewhere and that gives it, I hope, a sense of place that the reader can visualise.

If it's impossible to visit a physical location, the internet is your friend. Google Streetview and satellite imagery are incredibly useful resources, and internet searches will probably yield a host of useful photographs and local information. Sometimes this level of street-by-street information extends back hundreds of years. www.pastvu.com, for example, is a Russian website that allows you to search available historical photographs on a map by date, so that you can find images for, say, a particular Moscow street in 1936. Sadly pastvu.com isn't very useful outside Russia, but the internet is full of similar resources, if not quite so specific.

CONTEXT

Whether your setting is contemporary, historical or invented, it's worth considering what is going on around your narrative, historically, socially and politically, and how this might affect both your characters and your story. Fiction tends to be about day-to-day details, but that doesn't mean that the bigger picture won't have some relevance to your novel and how you want to tell it – being aware of what's going on around your story may suggest interesting historical themes, as well as offer possible avenues for your story to explore. If you consider your story with this wider view, you may well also find contemporary themes and resonances. A novel that revolves around a sexual assault on a young woman in the past will still be relevant to the present and even though the handling of the incident by the police and the reaction of her neighbours and family may be very different historically than they would be today, there may also be depressing similarities. If you are writing a contemporary novel about the same subject matter, you might find it useful to consider how sexual assaults would have been handled in the woman's mother's or grandmother's generation. There may, by way of example, be a generational gap between what older and younger people consider to be appropriate and inappropriate behaviour, and about their attitudes to publicising such an event.

If your story revolves around controversial issues, take the time to discover all points of view on the issue, even if they include opinions and attitudes you profoundly disagree with. If you have characters who have conflicting views, their discussions and conflicts will make your story more interesting and complex.

Consider also whether you really know the context of your story as well as you think you do. There will often be characters in your novel that have very different backgrounds and live very different lives to yours. It is worth taking the time to understand a little bit more about the practicalities of their day-to-day existence, what their motivations are and what worries and excites them. A very privileged person will have a significantly different set of daily concerns and experiences to someone who is homeless and unsure of where their next meal is coming from. If you're going to write such a character, make the effort to find out about them. What do they do for enjoyment? Where do they live? What do they eat? Where do they shop? What do they buy? What kind of relationships do they have with authority? What are their politics? What do they hope for from the future? If your character likes a particular song, does that signify something about them? When developing a character, it's really important to place them accurately in their environment if you want them to be convincing. More on character development in Chapter 4.

Similarly, if you are writing about people from a different country, religion or culture, take the time to discover as much as you can about them. If you are a man writing from the perspective of a female character, would it be sensible to have a woman read it for you to ensure you aren't making basic mistakes or noticing things, like the fact that they have breasts, which a woman would take for granted. When writers superimpose their view of the world on characters from backgrounds that are very different to theirs, it can make the characters unconvincing, and perhaps even offensive. In addition, it may well be your character's differences that lead to the conflicts and misunderstandings that will be useful to your story. While you should certainly establish the sensitivities that may exist when writing about different groups, you will also find that your research shapes the approach you take to your story in other ways, perhaps suggesting alternative characters, motivations and even storyline. For example, when researching the valley in Silesia where my novel *The Constant Soldier* was set, I discovered that there had been a mixed population of ethnic Germans, Poles and Jews living alongside each other for hundreds of years. At the beginning of World War II, the Poles and Jews were either murdered or expelled, and at the end of the war, the ethnic Germans were exiled in their turn. In other words, the Nazi's actions led, directly and indirectly, to the eradication of much of the valley's population and history and this trauma is something that I explore in the novel.

It's often easier to look at the context in which an historical novel takes place because it is, to a certain extent, fixed. Because contemporary life moves quickly when it comes to technology, politics, fashions and just about everything else, it is possible for novels to become dated even before publication and it is often difficult to create a fictional world that will continue to have the same relationship to reality that you intended at the time of writing. Phone technology, for example, has changed out of all recognition in the last fifteen years and while Covid is something very much at the forefront of my mind as I'm writing this, I've no idea what our view of Covid will be in three months' time, let alone in three years. Our views of the past change, but not as quickly as our experience of the present.

While you certainly want to be aware of what is going on at a global or national level in history, that kind of context may not actually feature very much in a historical novel, but it will provide a backdrop. If your historical central character is an important national figure or is involved in significant events, then you will need to be aware of the wider historical context. For example, if you set a novel in London in 1941, it would be odd if you didn't mention the Blitz, even if the novel is largely domestic in nature. Likewise, the adventures of a naval captain in 1805 will probably benefit from your being well informed as to the wider political and military context.

In other stories, the nation-level aspects of history may not be what you are looking for. Instead you will be more interested in the attitudes to morality and religion that existed, how communities worked on all levels, how justice was administered, where and how people shopped and worked and all kinds of other information on the practicalities of life. If you are writing about a period in the past, discovering people's day-to-day realities and attitudes will be the key to delivering that feeling of authenticity that readers expect. This knowledge should allow you to create characters who belong in the place and period, as opposed to characters with modern attitudes and behaviours who will read as being out of place.

For example, an openly gay character in sixteenth-century London is certainly possible but you will probably need to understand the restrictions that the period placed upon gay people and the strategies they would have used to circumvent them in order for the character and their story to be credible. The good news is that, provided you give them this credibility, having a character who is completely at odds with their surroundings is a great starting place for a novel, meaning that almost every aspect of their life becomes a challenge that they will have to overcome or work around. Similarly, an eighteenth-century female character might have very modern views on, say, equality between the sexes. However, in order for her to be convincing within the period, you would probably need to explain to the reader how limited women's rights were at the time and the reasons why your character has come to their very different views. Because you have done this research, your character's position, when expressed, will probably create conflict with the other characters, such as friends, family and persons in authority, as well as having other negative consequences for their social life. This is again going to provide your central character with obstacles and challenges which she will need to overcome before she achieves her final goal in the story. You may also find that your research suggests interesting parallels with our own times that you may want to explore. A novel about child labour in nineteenth-century Birmingham might find echoes in the young age of factory workers in some developing nations.

Aside from understanding your characters and how they will interact with each other and the world around them, bear in mind that historical fiction (and indeed all fiction with a setting unfamiliar to the reader) is a little like travel writing. Part of the attraction for the reader is that they want to experience this other place and time through the eyes of the characters you create. This means that you are also looking for sources that bring the past to life. Although I mentioned images as being a good basis for recreating physical locations, if examined carefully they can also explain how the world works. Opposite is an image of two World War I soldiers that I purchased for a World War I project I was researching. I know nothing about the photograph other than the fact that on the back of the image is written 'Uncle Fred and Uncle Stanley, 1917', who I presume are the two men in the photograph. At first sight, it might be thought that is all the information that the photograph has to yield.

On closer examination, however, the photograph reveals a little bit more about the two men and about the life of an ordinary soldier in World War I. Firstly, they have different cap badges, which probably indicates they were in different regiments. That's interesting, but in Stanley's case the badge is the only one of his brass fittings which is shiny, in contrast to Fred's which are all gleaming. I think this means that Fred's role was in the rear, whereas Stanley usually operated in the front lines where a shiny badge or button would have been a target for

Uncle Fred and Uncle Stanley, 1917

a sniper. In addition, if you look at the cleanliness of their uniforms, Stanley's is filthy which is consistent with his spending time in the trenches. It also reminds us that, unlike in many films of World War I, where the uniforms are relatively clean, the reality of trench warfare would have been that soldiers were literally caked in mud for most of their time in the front line, with no change of uniform until they were relieved. Another interesting difference between the two men is the shape of their caps. Stanley's has had the stiffener taken out of it, perhaps so that it could be worn under a steel helmet, whereas Fred's has not. Both men look exhausted, which is probably to be expected and, for me anyway, tells us something about the stress and living conditions under which they operated. One final thing to notice is that the backdrop is probably painted, and the photograph taken in a studio by one of the many commercial photographers who plied their trade in the rear area and printed their photographs as postcards, of which this is one. Perhaps when it was taken, neither Fred not Stanley thought they would see their family again, and this photograph was intended to memorialise them.

Other sources which can be revealing are letters, memoirs, diaries and even fiction from the period, as well as more academic histories. Newspapers are also treasure troves of the kind of information you're looking for and it's worth paying attention to the classified sections and any advertising. These will tell about local hostelries and meeting places, as well as the medical ailments and 'cures' that were current and what it cost to hire an under-gardener. Don't forget to also seek out the everyday objects which people would have used, many of which can be found in specialist and local museums. You're looking for anything that can bring the physical sense of being in the time and place, and then attempting to communicate it to the reader.

INSIDE KNOWLEDGE AND MORE FOCUSSED RESEARCH

Aside from details about locations and more general social and contextual research, you may find there is information specific to your novel that you will have to find a way of uncovering (if you don't know it already). For example, if you are setting a novel in a coal mine, or on a fishing boat, you will probably quickly discover that each setting has specialist equipment, technical language and ways of doing things that are unique to them. The authenticity of your novel will benefit from including at least some of these elements. So how do you go about acquiring this knowledge?

Of course, the best approach is to go and spend time in the specialist environment that you are hoping to write about. So, if you want to recreate life on a fishing boat, try and find a way of experiencing that life first hand – if only for a few hours. The good news is that you will find that most people are intrigued by the novel-writing process and, within reason, surprisingly willing to help a novelist with research when approached. Obviously, some environments are less open to visitors than others and if you're setting your novel in the headquarters of MI5, you may struggle. However, it's always worth asking and most large organisations have websites and an email to a press officer will often yield surprising results. Even if you aren't able to get access, a little bit of digging should put you in contact with someone who has most of the information you require. Work out the type of person you need to talk to and, if you can identify a suitable prospect, approach them directly; alternatively, if no one suitable is immediately accessible, attempt contact through professional organisations, unions or even Facebook groups and bulletin boards. A polite message can work wonders and, if there is any sensitivity, be sure to agree with your source in advance how you will use the information.

Crime writing offers a good example of the importance of this kind of research. Authors of crime novels are generally very careful to do quite a lot of research into the police, criminals, the court system, the prison system and how criminal investigations are run, then use it to recreate a convincing version of that reality. If you're writing a contemporary novel that involves a particular police force, unless you've worked at the organisation in question, you're probably going to need to become familiar with their procedures, approaches to evidence-gathering and interviewing techniques. You should also ensure you have a good grasp of the forensic technology available to investigators. TV documentaries and crime dramas will give plenty of general insights into contemporary law enforcement in an easily accessible format but other sources might include police internet forums, personal contacts, published memoirs, criminology textbooks, case histories, trial transcripts and newspaper reports. As always, personal experience is best, but if not, get as close as you can through individual sources or other research.

If you do receive help from a particular person, organisation or other source, you should always show your gratitude both personally, and in the acknowledgements of your novel if it is published. Not only is an acknowledgement something that sources appreciate, but it shows the reader that you have done your research. Bear in mind, however, that if the information you have been given is sensitive or confidential, then your source may not want to be mentioned in any identifiable way. In addition, it is always polite to acknowledge a source's usefulness, while mentioning that any errors are your own.

Finding out information about equipment that your characters may need to use, but which you are unfamiliar with, can also be a challenge although not an insurmountable one. As always, if you can find some way of using the equipment yourself, do so. Experiencing something yourself is always the best place from which to recreate it in your novel. If you have never held a sword, it is going to be much more difficult to write about than if you have. That said, sometimes getting your hands on the real thing can be difficult and sometimes even illegal. Weapons, in particular, are something you might want to research but may find it is somewhat tricky in the UK, where guns and other weapons can be comparatively difficult to access. To compound the problem, there are a surprisingly large number of readers, particularly in the US, who seem to know more about lethal weapons than seems healthy for the rest of the population, and who aren't afraid to leave an Amazon review to tell you exactly what you have got wrong (as I know from experience). It may be possible, if your novel is historical, to access decommissioned or replica weapons through re-enactment groups: there are, again, websites and bulletin boards devoted to them that will put you in touch with enthusiasts for almost any period or place, who are not only expert on the weapons you may need to know about but also a great deal of other useful information. If you are interested in a more contemporary weapon, you'll find that thousands of technical videos have been uploaded to YouTube by gun-owners demonstrating details of almost every weapon you might conceivably want to know about. (Not to mention the hundreds of internet forums filled with gun-owners, who are only too pleased to share their expertise.) If you have any concerns about the depth of your knowledge, my advice – gained again from personal experience – is to avoid being too specific. As soon as you go into the details of how you load or clean a particular weapon, you run the risk of an inadvertent inaccuracy.

Although firearms present their own problems, the general approach of either trying to get first-hand experience or finding someone who has that first-hand experience *and* is willing to help you, is generally the one to take when looking at any other modern equipment or technology. Historical technology may be a little more difficult, but if you can't find a re-enactment group or museum to assist, other historians, experts and collectors may be able to do so. If the knowledge you are looking for is related to manufacturing or a craft, you may find that there are social historians and museums who specialise in the area; guilds and craft associations may also have useful knowledge, and written sources (either recent or from the time you are looking at) could offer key insights.

THE NATURAL WORLD

One area that is often overlooked by writers is the natural world. If you mention any kind of plant or animal life, it's worth double-checking that it is found in the place you're writing about, at the time of year you've set the scene and whether it will be in the condition you have described. Flowers that are in bloom in mid-winter are rare, deciduous trees probably won't have leaves and, likewise, some animals hibernate, migrate or change their behaviour in other ways. I'm not a great expert on plant life but many readers are and naming trees and other flora can give them a very clear visual image, so it's a good idea to give these details if at all possible. I have an app on my phone called *Picture This* which identifies most plants from images I take (generally accurately). There are plenty of similar resources for animal and bird life.

You should also double-check the weather: is it correct for the time of year? I have read a novel set in the Southern Hemisphere that didn't take account of the seasons being different to the Northern Hemisphere. If it's relevant, remember that daylight hours vary throughout the year and depending on geographical position.

When you're writing about a different historical period, again, you have to be careful – tomatoes, tobacco and potatoes, for example, are relative newcomers to Europe (they were unknown before Europeans sailed to America in the sixteenth century) and many of the animals we now accept as typical may have been unknown at the time you're writing about, or may have changed substantially in the intervening years. It's also worth thinking about the climate – the modern European winter is far milder than it was in the seventeenth century, when it was common for the Thames to freeze over. This isn't just a detail when you realise that, in an era before central heating and running water, consistent temperatures of 10 or 15 degrees Celsius below zero would have had a significant impact on the way people led their lives. Therefore, you will need to adapt your characters to suit the environment and setting; though you would be surprised by the number of authors who don't.

THE PRACTICALITIES OF RESEARCH

Make the most of your research time – particularly if it's limited – by preparing well. For example, if you are visiting a city for three days to research it as a location, or a museum to look at particular objects, identify your priorities – the things you absolutely have to see or experience – and schedule your time accordingly. As mentioned above, taking photographs (where possible) is sensible, especially as images are both accurate records of what you see but also serve as a reminder of details that can't be photographed. Taking notes, particularly of those non-visual details that you want to recall, can be more time-consuming and, if you are really pressed for time, can be done afterwards. If you have limited time in a library, again taking photographs of documents, if allowed, can be far quicker than reading them and taking notes.

Preparation is also vital if you are interviewing someone. Ask their permission to record the interview so you don't miss anything and don't get slowed down by taking notes. Be sure to work out your questions in advance so that you obtain all of the information that you need and later on make a transcript of the recording so that you can refer to it more easily.

Much of your research will be done online or through reading. If you are doing a lot of research for a novel, over a long period of time, you may find that your notes soon mount up. I generally try and catalogue them using Word documents and image folders. When I was researching Moscow in the 1930s for my first three novels, I created folders of photographs showing Moscow cultural events, and included where possible the date, location and the name of the photographer or copyright owner in case I needed to reproduce it at some stage. If I found something interesting in a Gulag memoir, I would make a note including the title of the memoir and the page it appeared on, and then catalogue it accordingly. My system allows me to find the information I need fairly easily. The key thing is that – whichever system you choose – it organises your research so that it is accessible and doesn't involve you having to reread books or trawl the internet again to rediscover a remembered image.

Handling research

Once you've done your research, the question is how you use it. You've probably heard other writers say that 99 per cent of the research that you do for a novel doesn't end up on the page, and that's probably true. Most of what you find won't be of direct use to your novel, either because it doesn't take the story forward or because including it will require an explanation that will slow the story down. Don't worry, all of that research has still been useful because it has made you confident in your subject matter and that confidence will communicate itself to the reader. I'm afraid it's often the case that you don't know whether you need to research something until you have actually researched it. While that sometimes means you can feel like you've wasted your time, on other occasions you'll find something that will improve your story dramatically. The question is, what research do you keep and how do you use it to help the story? Is there a detail that will help the plot, or give the reader an image of the setting or a feeling of authenticity?

DON'T RESEARCH TOO MUCH

Despite all I've said above, you are writing fiction, so don't become so caught up in researching your novel, that you forget to write it. Try and decide what you need to have for the story and limit yourself to that. If an interesting line of research doesn't push your story forward, it will probably have to be jettisoned before the final draft, so bear that in mind.

DON'T LET RESEARCH STIFLE YOUR STORY

Successful novels engage and entertain the reader – at the very least; they often do lots more – and sometimes research can get in the way of that. You want to provide a convincing and consistent world within which your story can take place, but that world is mostly going to be the *background* to your story, rather than the story itself. Your objective is to convince the reader that you know what you're talking about but that doesn't mean you should spend several pages talking about the origins of computing, fascinating as that might be, or why two people can't have the same DNA or fingerprints. Unless you're writing about something that is completely incomprehensible without explanation, then your best approach is to allow your readers to fill in the blanks. Your story is predominately about the characters and what they do and why, and if your research features too strongly, it will slow your story down.

Think of your reader as being someone who lives in the time and place that you're writing about, or someone who has similar experience and knowledge to your characters. This imaginary reader won't need, or expect, to have many things explained to them. It may sound counter-intuitive but most readers are very happy reading a novel written 200 years ago, precisely because it doesn't waste time explaining how society worked but just goes ahead and shows it. Likewise, they won't need to know how your character loads that rare Czech pistol, just whether it hits the target or not. And if you use terminology and processes that are authentic while describing a surgeon operating on a patient, you won't need to go into exact detail for the reader to accept that your depiction is accurate and for them to be able to have a good image of what is going on. Similarly, when I am describing a place I often start with a wide angle description – 'A small cottage stood in front of him'. – and then look for one or two details that will bring that very bland image to life for the reader. For example: 'Chimney smoke trailed upwards from its thatched roof.' I could give much more description, but the reader has enough to create a mental image and unless there is something about the exterior of the cottage that is significant to my story, such as a broken window from a break in, I can move on.

There are, of course, exceptions: if your novel is about counterfeiting, you may need to explain the mechanics of currency distribution because it is key to the plot. However, in many cases, the best research is the research you leave off the page.

DON'T LET RESEARCH GET IN THE WAY OF YOUR STORY

Sometimes you'll reach a place in your story where you would like something to happen, but your research probably suggests it wouldn't. For example, in crime fiction, police detectives often interview suspects in public places without cautioning them and often indulge in other behaviour that might make the police's professional standards authorities weep with frustration. Although it's nice to be accurate, remember (again) that you are writing fiction and your readers expect to be entertained. If every fictional police interview took place in a police station, with cautioning and tape recordings and lawyers present, then it might be a little repetitive so you are allowed to skip over some details and ignore others if it helps the story.

If your novel is about real people and real events, whether in the past or present, you may find your research will only go so far and that there are conversations and interactions that you just have to imagine, or invent. If you are writing about the distant past and if you have done your research well and understand the people involved, your inventions will probably be credible and, if you acknowledge your inventions in an afterword, you're unlikely to cause much offence. You need to be much more careful when your subjects are still living, however. Aside from the risk of libelling them, there may also be wider sensitivities, and obvious inventions may put your novel in a difficult position. In this case, while your story can be *based on* real events, it's probably best to fictionalise everything – changing locations, names and even incidents – to be on the safe side.

BEWARE THE INACCURATE ACCURACY

The purpose of research is largely to create a credible environment for your story to take place within. With this in mind, even when you're right about a fact or an event, the reader might think you're wrong. How? Well, occasionally you'll discover things through research that go against commonly held opinion or presumption and it's tempting to use them in your novel. Be careful, however, the last thing you want is for a reader to step out of the flow of your novel to go and check something or – even worse – carry on reading, but believing you are mistaken and thus being more inclined to second-guess other elements of your novel. My view? Unless the fact is key to your narrative, I would avoid using it: the story – and maintaining your reader's engagement – always takes priority.

Summary

HOW TO RESEARCH

- Always visit the location or locations you are writing about and consider the following:
  - How will your scenes work within the existing surroundings and architecture?
    - How will the scene work practically?

        - Where will the characters be placed, and how will the action proceed?
        - How many other people are around, and how will this affect the action?
    - How will the weather, time of day and season impact on the location?
        - What flora and fauna are in the location, and how will they look at the time of year your story is set?
    - Are there any unusual or interesting features you can use to give a strong sense of place?
    - Imagine your characters within the space:
        - How will they see the location: is it familiar or new to them?
        - What will they notice about the location?
        - How does your character feel in the location?
        - What will they need to know about the location? E.g. are there any challenges that the space presents to them?
    - Take photographs and make notes about anything you may want to use in your writing. This includes street names, buildings, landmarks and anything that specifically identifies the location.
    - Use resources such as maps, old photographs, paintings and sketches of the location to identify buildings or features that may no longer exist but may be relevant to your story.
    - Identify any local customs or festivals that may be specific to the location.
- Look at sources from your chosen historical period (if applicable) such as images, letters, memoirs and newspapers.

- Where appropriate, spend time in specialist environments to understand the processes your character may need to carry out. Doing activities in-person is best to inform your writing.
  - Is there any technical equipment, language or practices that can be used in your novel?
  - Speak to people with first-hand experience that is related to the specialism you are researching.
- Make use of local and specialist libraries, archives and museums.

  Contact professional organisations and unions, and use the internet and social media, to tap into others' knowledge.

CONTEXT

- Consider the historical, social and political framework of your chosen setting:
  - How will it affect the characters and story?
  - As you write, you need to be aware of what is happening more broadly within society, even if it does not feature heavily within the novel.
- Consider all of the points of view characters may have on issues, especially on controversial or contentious subjects. You may not agree with a particular point of view, but to ignore it altogether does not paint an accurate picture of society.
- When writing characters who are from a different background to yours – whether social-economic, ethnic group, religious or cultural – take time to research and understand the practicalities of their day-to-day lives and experiences.
  - Talk to someone from the same background you're writing about to help you build an authentic and accurate character. If not researched properly, you may end up using out-dated and offensive stereotypes.

HANDLING RESEARCH

- Be prepared.
  - Have your camera and notebook with you when visiting locations.
  - Prepare interview questions in advance and record the interview if you are permitted.
- Catalogue your research (including typing up written notes and making transcripts of interviews).
  - Use folders on your computer and name files appropriately.
  - Include all source information, including copyright information if applicable. This may be just the book title and a page number, but it should allow you to easily find the source material again.
- Place your research in context. It is important, but so is your story, so only include the pieces of research that will drive that story forward.
- Think of the reader as someone who lives in the time and place you are writing about. This will limit the amount of explanation you will need to include.
- Research can only provide so much; there will be things you will still need to imagine or invent to make your story work.

CHAPTER 4

Central characters

Most novels have a clearly identifiable central character and a story that revolves around that character's efforts to achieve an objective, whether that be to climb Mount Everest, reconcile with a parent or be united with their beloved. When a novel has a clear central character the story is, in essence, *their* story. The other characters, to a large extent, exist to either help or hinder the central character's journey towards their objective, or to tell us something about the central character as a person. As a result, the novel will often be told mostly or completely from the central character's point of view, and if there are other storytelling points of view, the central character will usually remain the story's focus. In fact, even if the central character isn't on a particular page or in a specific chapter, the story is almost certain to remain focussed on the central character and their journey through the novel.

Just as the central character is at the heart of the novel's story, they are also fundamental to its success; if they aren't a successful creation then that will have an effect on the reader's engagement with the novel. In this chapter we will consider the central character's roles, the decisions that a writer needs to make about them and the questions they need to ask of them in order to ensure that your central character will hold the reader's attention until the very last page.

Some novels, of course, have two central characters – my own 2018 novel, *A House of Ghosts*, is one such – while other novels focus on a *group* of characters, as is the case in the *Song of Fire and Ice* series by George R. R. Martin. Generally, in these situations, the dual central characters or the group of characters will be bound together in some way that, because of the connection, makes their *shared* story the subject of the novel. A romantic novel, for example might split the story and storytelling responsibilities between two would-be lovers.

Although in this chapter we will be considering a novel with a single central character, almost everything can be applied to novels which tell the story of two central characters and, indeed, to novels about a group. Essentially, a group or shared central characters operate similarly in story terms to how a single central character operates.

Before we get into more detail, however, let's consider what the central character does in a novel.

THEY DRIVE THE STORY

The story is *their* story. In other words, the story won't take place, or at least not in the same way, without their decisions and actions. The story will almost always be about the central character's struggle to achieve *their* objective, whether that's to climb a mountain or kill a dragon or be elected president. Much of the story, therefore, will be about the central character overcoming challenges and obstacles that we, the writers, will place between them and that objective. Those obstacles and challenges will often involve the central character being in conflict with the other characters, the setting or themselves, which means that the central character should be capable of creating that conflict, often because we place them in opposition to the other characters or the setting, or because we give them an internal flaw or dilemma that they will need to address. Our central character, in other words, needs to be active in the story and if the story needs direction or momentum, they will be the character we will look to for the action or decision that will move the story forward or increase its pace.

THEY TELL THE STORY

More often than not, the central character will provide the sole or predominant storytelling voice. The novel is the central character's story, so it makes sense that we use their perspective to tell it. While a single central character novel may be told entirely from the central character's point of view, it is also common (and useful), to use alternative storytelling points of view as well. While such a novel may use multiple storytelling points of view, it will probably be the case that the central character's storytelling voice will take up the majority of the storytelling duties. Indeed, even where we use another character to narrate a scene, they will often be observing the central character who will remain the focus of the scene. Because so much of the storytelling is likely to be done by the central character, and your novel will probably be several hundred pages long, you will need to ensure the character is capable of telling the story well and that they can do that in an entertaining or interesting way.

THEY ENGAGE THE READER'S ATTENTION

Even if your central character is active within the story and capable of telling the story in an appealing way, it is still crucial that the reader engages with them on an emotional level. If that doesn't happen, the novel may well struggle to hold their attention. That doesn't mean that your reader has to like your central character, just that they have to care about them and what they are trying to achieve.

Building a central character

When you start to develop a central character, you may only have a very hazy idea of their personality and appearance. You may have a name, know their sex and age and perhaps a little about their background but it is always worth spending time thinking about and expanding on them. For our purposes, let's begin at the beginning and develop two different characters, one female and one male: Sybil is a 73-year-old retired scientist and Wayne a 25-year-old lawyer. Nearly everything that happens in any novel featuring these characters will happen either as result of their actions and decisions, be constrained by their abilities and personality, or be shaped by their personality and agenda. Each detail of their personality, appearance or situation will be important for the story. For example, if they are attractive and charming (or the opposite), it will affect their relationships with other characters. If you know who they care about, and to what extent, then this may provide useful motivation for their behaviour at key moments in the story. Knowing what their particular abilities and strengths are will be important to the story, as will knowing any weaknesses and flaws.

Before you start writing your central character, therefore, it is sensible to find out as much as you can about them. This may sound slightly strange, given they are your fictional creation, but the fact that they are fictional and created by you means that your central character only exists to the extent that you have thought about them, and therefore the more thinking you do, the more realised they will become. To put it another way, the more questions you ask, the more answers you will receive and the more fictional flesh you will put on their fictional bones. Where to begin, however?

FIRST IMPRESSIONS

When we meet someone for the first time in real life, we often make assumptions about their personality based on their appearance and how they carry themselves. It is the same for readers (and indeed the other characters) when it comes to your central character. With this in mind, it is important to consider, and be in control of, the external impression your central character presents. On a purely practical basis, it's easier to write and develop a character if you have a very clear image in your mind of what they look like (even if you may deliberately decide to withhold some or all of that image from the reader). If you know how they appear to the other characters and what impression they create, then you have an idea of how the other characters will react to them, and vice versa.

When choosing a character's external identity, however, you need to think through the implications. If readers, and the other characters in the novel, have preconceptions based on your central character's appearance, that can be a useful shorthand for you to suggest their personality – although, of course, you can also use those preconceptions to mislead. Your reader might be surprised, for example, if a central character who looks like a heavyweight boxer turns out to work as a jewellery designer. In a similar way, elements of your central character's appearance may provoke strong reactions from the other characters. The jewellery designer who looks like a boxer will probably, despite his best intentions, seem intimidating to other characters. Similarly, an attractive woman may find herself the subject of unwanted attention from male characters and may not be taken as seriously as she should be in a professional context. Some characters may attempt to deliberately mislead with their appearance. An undertaker may dress soberly at work but be a very different person in their private life. In your story, their private life may be something they would prefer to keep secret and this preference may be key to what transpires.

Not every novel gives a clear description of the central character's physical appearance. Sometimes this is because the novel is told solely from their point of view and it can feel contrived for the central character to describe themselves to the reader. However, there are many scenes in novels where characters gaze at themselves in mirrors (at least one of which was written by me). It is also the case that some authors prefer to leave the reader to create their own image of the central character. However, even if you decide to hold back your central character's appearance, it is sensible for you, as the writer of your novel, to have a clear image of them because their appearance affects many of the interactions with the other characters. In order to help with this, I often begin the process of creating a central character by trying to find a photograph of someone that I think may be similar in appearance to how I imagine them. I use the photograph as a starting point rather than a template, and I find it a very useful basis on which to build the character. A lot of that building happens when I ask myself questions, often along the lines of the following:

How old are they?

Readers, like everyone else, will have preconceptions about a character based on their age. They may find it easier to think of a younger character as being impetuous, naïve, or energetic whereas they may associate frailty, conservative beliefs and caution with an older character. Obviously, you can undermine those assumptions but, if you have flexibility as to the age of your character, it is worth considering what those assumptions are and if they may be useful. If Wayne, our lawyer, is a young, fit man, we immediately have some idea of what he might be capable of physically, but his age and physical condition, particularly if he looks younger than he actually is, may cause him to be underestimated intellectually by his colleagues. It may be tempting to present Sybil, who is older and a woman, as a kindly grandmother, but that may be not be the kind of character we need. Giving her an intimidating stare and a sense that she doesn't suffer fools gladly doesn't mean that she can't have a softer side as well.

Are they male or female?

Again, readers may have expectations of your central character based on their sex, particularly when it is combined with other elements such as age, background and physical appearance. An expectation from the reader that a central character will play a passive role in the story based on their sex is unlikely to be an accurate one. Your central character will be the driving force for your narrative so they may have attributes – including resilience, determination, bravery and intelligence – that will enable them to be that even if their interactions with the other characters may be affected by their sex and other factors.

How tall are they?

A shorter character may face physical challenges that a taller character may not, and vice versa. Also consider how your reader, and the other characters in the novel, may react to the central character's height. If Wayne is only a smidgen over 5 feet, that could work both for him and against him. Likewise, if Sybil is close to six feet tall, then her physical presence may be more commanding but it may also make life difficult for her physically, and her height may be slightly off-putting to a romantic prospect who is shorter. At the same time, some novels may require a central character of a certain appearance. A tall, dark and handsome man might work well for a romance novel while a novel about basketball may require height as an attribute.

What is their body shape?

A character's weight may have implications for their physical strength and health. If the central character has a job or is engaged in an activity that requires a particular body shape, will it be useful to have them not comply with expectations? If a policeman is exceptionally tall, will the other characters react positively or negatively, and will those reactions be justified, or misplaced? Will your central character need to be physically fit to achieve the tasks that you will set them over the course of the novel and how will you establish this? If our story involves physical activity for Wayne, making him unfit could make the challenges he faces that bit more difficult. If Sybil is thin, that may be due to illness or to healthy living – which one might be more useful in story terms? If an unfit Wayne is romantically interested in a very athletic woman, have we created an obstacle for him to overcome?

Is the central character physically attractive, or otherwise?

If a character is beautiful, other characters may react more positively than they would otherwise. The other characters may believe that a certain kind of attractiveness implies positive character traits such as honesty, empathy and kindness – although obviously that may not be the case. On the other hand, a superficially unattractive central character may have all of these qualities and more, although the other characters may need to discover this over the course of the novel. Might these misconceptions be useful for your story? When you are considering the attractiveness and appearance of your central character, it can often be useful to place them at a disadvantage. An attractive woman may find herself the object of both wanted and unwanted attention. How will she deal with this? I think we should presume that Sybil has aged relatively well, but her attractiveness may not be immediately visible to those who don't know her. Wayne on the other hand, could have a round, innocent face that is not a reflection of his true, much more complex, personality.

How do they dress? Are they well groomed?

If your character takes pride in their appearance, that may imply care, wealth and creativity, although it may also be used to suggest superficiality. If, on the other hand, they do not care much about their personal appearance and dress in whatever comes to hand, that may imply disorganisation or perhaps even self-confidence. Clothes may also reflect status and occupation – and whether they will be appropriate for your central character. I suspect Sybil will dress in a contemporary manner, with a certain style, suggesting she is young at heart and sophisticated. Wayne may choose tee shirts and shorts when he isn't in the office, but wear tailored suits when he is. This may indicate that he is ambivalent about his career, or at least, that he doesn't let it define his private persona.

How does your central character speak?

How your central character speaks to other characters will come from the personality you have created for them and their situation. For example, if you want them to be confident and forceful, that will be reflected in the words you choose for them and how they speak them. However, your character may well speak differently to a child, an elderly relative and a colleague, respectively. As in everyday life, your central character will probably adjust their speech to their audience but remain consistent in essence. If they don't adjust, that probably tells us something about their personality. That said, it is often useful to create points of difference between your central character and the characters that surround them. Having your central character speak with a foreign accent, or an accent that implies a different social background, may create misunderstanding, suspicion or even enmity. Wayne may be hard of hearing, which causes him to speak loudly in abrupt, short sentences. Sybil may have a working-class accent and a line in colourful imagery. In both cases, the way they speak may affect their relationships with other characters.

Do they have a disability or other health challenge?

From a story point of view, a disability will probably present a challenge to your central character that they will have to overcome.

As with Wayne being hard of hearing, a disabled character may see or experience the world in a very different light to someone without a disability, and face different challenges and obstacles. This will be interesting for the reader if handled well. Depending on the disability, you may have story constraints or opportunities which may help you or need to be worked around. If their disability is one which the central character wants to hide, such as an artificial limb – might this provide an aspect to their story that will add a little complexity. Finally, the character's disability – and how they deal with it – may shape the reader's engagement with them in a positive way. How might you make certain that happens with Wayne?

Is there something unusual about their physical appearance?
If your central character has a facial scar, is missing a finger or has an impressive dragon tattoo, it will suggest to the reader something about their present situation or their past. If a character has a scar, for example, and you don't tell the reader about its origin immediately but hint that it is significant to the story, then that suspended question may encourage the reader to read on to find out exactly what that significance might be. This is an option that you should use relatively rarely, but if Sybil has a Mohican haircut, it will certainly mean she is seen in a different light by the reader and the other characters.

Are they racially or ethnically different to the other characters?
Being different in some way is often part of the job description for a central character. Being racially or ethnically different can create all kinds of challenges and obstacles for the central character, particularly where the other characters are hostile or reluctant to engage with them. A character facing obstacles related to the their race or ethnicity may well have a more meaningful and significant story. If there are certain issues and attitudes that you want to explore around race or ethnicity, having a character from a particular background may be essential. However, dealing with such differences will require careful thought and sensitivity, particularly if you are not from that racial or ethnic background.

What is their name?

Wayne and Sybil are good enough character names to start with but I often change my mind about a name several times while writing a novel, and then change it again following an editorial suggestion. The likelihood is that your final choice will say something about your character's nature, background and aspirations. Charles Dickens chose names that were often explicit character descriptions – Scrooge, for example. Contemporary novelists tend to be more restrained but while Ian Rankin's detective John Rebus is a more subtle choice, the association with puzzles and blood types is certainly useful for a detective.

Where do they come from?

Your central character will have had a past before the moment when you introduce them to your readers and often it will provide them with the incentive for their being part of the story, or be the basis for the story itself. For example, it's not unusual in crime novels that the crime will have a particular resonance to the detective because of something in their past. If, for example, the detective has lost a loved one to a killer and finds themselves investigating a case that has close parallels, it will probably be useful motivation. The detective may know that a different killer is to blame, but solving this murder may help them come to terms with the loss and guilt they may feel at having failed to prevent the murder of their loved one. Likewise, if a detective returns to a town that she left under a cloud, solving a local crime may be a path to redemption for a perceived wrongdoing and might also reconnect them with a family and community that has rejected them.

The central character's back story will reveal elements of their personality and how it has been shaped. It will also be relevant to how they see the world, and how the world sees them. If Wayne, our young lawyer, grew up in poverty and had brushes with the law in his youth, that may make him empathise with victims of social injustice and be the reason why he became a lawyer. Alternatively, it may have made him determined to climb the social and career ladder at any cost. If he grew up on a council estate in Edinburgh, he may feel out of place in a London workplace where most of his colleagues are from privileged English backgrounds. On the other hand, it may also be that this background has given him skills and adaptability that make him unique.

Similarly, if Sybil worked as a research scientist for much of her life, she may see the world in a very precise, analytical light but she may also notice things that other people don't. She may also have something in her past that she needs to address in some way – a ruptured relationship that she would like to rekindle or a secret hurt that she would like to confront. If Sybil was a refugee from political turmoil in her youth, she might feel a connection with a younger refugee that others would not.

If you construct an interesting and relevant background for your central character, the question is when should you reveal it? It's often a good idea to not reveal information of this kind too early, particularly when its later revelation will change the reader's perception of the central character, and indeed the entire story. Sometimes the revelation will come in the form of a twist, but it's not essential that it comes as a big surprise to the reader. You can leave small clues and make occasional suggestions that let the reader know that there is something in the central character's past that is relevant. These clues and suggestions will get the reader thinking and asking questions, which should mean the reader is engaged, which is a very good thing.

What is their current situation?

You will also need to think about where you place your central character in your fictional world and what is their personal situation. What do they do for a living? What is their general state of mind? Who are their friends and loved ones? Have they a particular enemy? Where do they live and in what degree of comfort? What are their pastimes and interests? The answer to each of these questions will indicate something about your central character's personality but also suggest ideas for how their story, and the novel's plot, can be shaped.

As always, we are often looking for ways in which we can create conflict for our central character and, with this in mind, it is worth looking at their surroundings and seeing if we can place them in conflict with them. For example, if you wanted to write a novel about undergraduate life at Oxford, you would probably have two very different novels depending on whether your central character feels they fit into that environment or, instead, feels out of place. Likewise, if your story is about a plane crash in the jungle, will the novel be more interesting if your central character is an experienced explorer or someone on their first overseas journey from a small Welsh village? If your central character is a fish out of water in the environment in which they find themselves, they will almost certainly face greater difficulties in achieving their objective and will also have to adapt and compromise in order to succeed. In addition, their being out of place will probably provide opportunities for humour and, even more importantly, because the world is strange to them, they will be able to naturally observe interesting details in a way that might seem clunky from a narrator who is familiar with the setting. So, let's ask some questions and see what we find out.

What do they do for a living?

We know that Sybil is retired and that Wayne works as a lawyer, which is a good start. If we are looking to create opportunities for our story, we could make them a little dissatisfied. Perhaps Wayne is from a very different background to his colleagues and is being overlooked for promotion despite deserving it. Likewise, if Sybil is bored with her retirement and is looking for something to occupy her, that could be an incentive for her becoming involved if an opportunity for adventure comes her way. Of course, what a central character does for a living may also suggest something to us about their personality. We will likely have different expectations of a firefighter and an author, although of course it may turn out that the author is an excellent firefighter when the occasion arises. You might also consider why the character has chosen their profession – is it something they love, or have they embarked on their career to please a parent. If the latter, they may be dissatisfied with the choice they've made. Also, think about how long they have been in their job. If it's a relatively short period, they will still be proving themselves to their colleagues and overcoming resistance. If it's a longer period, maybe they are looking for a new challenge or are ambitious for advancement.

What is their general state of mind?

I try to look for a defining characteristic here, and then think about the implications. Your character can be happy or sad, excited or bored, contented or discontented, optimistic or pessimistic or one of hundreds of other possibilities. In each case, their state of mind will tell us something about their personality and perhaps also cause us to empathise with them. If Sybil is unhappy with her surroundings and expresses it through a sharp, dry humour, that may make us like her as a character, as well as annoying those around her in the novel. If Wayne remains optimistic in the face of persistent unfair bias, we may admire him for his determination and Wayne's optimism may also eventually win over the other characters. If the defining characteristic is a negative one, the story may be about changing it to a positive one.

Who are their friends and loved ones?

Conflict often comes from people having different opinions or wanting different outcomes and these can be expressed without confrontation, although the conflict can result in that as well. The discussion that ensues, in whatever form it takes, and the decisions or compromises that are reached as a result of it, however, can be the whole essence of a novel. If Sybil has a son who is determined to put her in a nursing home, even though she doesn't need to be in one, he may be motivated by concern for her but he may also benefit from the change. Placing the two of them in conflict over this issue may force them to find some middle ground and perhaps also to address other issues within their relationship.

Friends and loved ones can also reveal the central character's personality. If Wayne stays loyal to old friends, the reader may think well of him for it; if he treats his girlfriend badly, we may think less of him for it. The friends our characters choose may also suggest qualities and faults in their own personality. If Sybil's friends are younger, that may indicate she is young at heart. If Sybil's friends are very intelligent, that probably implies something similar about her.

Friends and loved ones can also be the central character's greatest allies when facing the challenges and obstacles that the story will present. A friend of Wayne's who advises and supports him in his attempts to advance in his career may be helpful, particularly when the friend puts minor obstacles in perspective or suggests solutions to problems. However, Wayne may have a different friend who is a bad influence, perhaps even involving him in illegal activity that threatens to destroy his career.

Friends and family can also be very useful towards the end of the novel. A risk to the central character's relationship with their spouse may be the motivation the central character needs to overcome the greatest challenge or achieve their final objective.

Have they a particular enemy?

The other side of the coin to a loved one is someone that the central character doesn't get on with. Your central character may be in a long-standing conflict with this person from before the start of the novel, or the ill feeling may emerge during the novel. A foe can provide the central character with motivation, conflict and challenges in a similar way to a friend. The enmity may be as a result of the characters being polar opposites, or perhaps because they are very similar; once the novel begins exploring the reasons behind the enmity, it will give the reader insights into the central character's personality. A central character doesn't have to have an enemy or rival, but it's often useful if they do because of the conflict and challenges the enmity will create. If, for example, Sybil has a twin sister who is the rival for a lover's affection, then the reason for their tense relationship may be as much about their shared past as it is about the attractiveness of the man in question but the antipathy and competition will make Sybil's progress through the novel more difficult.

How do they interact with the other characters?

It is also worth considering how you want your character to get on with the characters that surround them in the novel. If everyone else in the novel is eccentric, perhaps your central character should be very straight-laced and therefore uncomfortable in their presence. If the other characters are very traditional, perhaps our central character should be the opposite with a sense of humour that goes too far (in their eyes at least). The more you can mark out your characters as the exception, the more useful this will be for you in terms of creating conflict but also in making opportunities for them to observe as well as go on a journey of mutual compromise and understanding.

Where do they live and in what degree of comfort?

If Sybil were to live in a tumbledown cottage at the end of a country lane, this would probably create a certain impression in the reader's mind. If she lives in a minimalist city-centre loft apartment, however, a completely different view of her would be created. It's worth thinking what impressions living arrangements will create and then considering how you can use them for your own purposes. Is it a shorthand way of telling the reader something about Sybil? Or is it also a way to mislead the reader ever so slightly, only to surprise them at a later stage? If Sybil is a recent arrival to the community in which she lives, how might that be useful? Or if she is instead very much at the heart of the local community, is that going to help your story in a different way?

What are their pastimes and interests?

What interests your central character? If they like going to the theatre, that tells the reader something about them, particularly if this seems inconsistent with their love of greyhound racing. The very modern loft apartment might say one thing about Sybil, but the fact that she loves going to football matches may indicate something else. If we have established Wayne as a high-powered lawyer, the fact that he paints to a very high standard in his time off might suggest hidden depths that the reader won't have expected. Giving your character a very strong religious belief, and making that important to the story, may place them in conflict with characters who have different beliefs or are militantly secular. It can be illuminating, when considering your central character, to 'ask them' a whole series of random questions. Do they like dogs, or cats, or neither? Will they cycle to work or walk? Do they prefer the mountains or the sea? Every detail you acquire about the central character will help you understand them better, as well as coming in useful for your story.

With a central character's backstory, you may want to hold elements of it in reserve until quite late in the novel, although you probably want to establish their current circumstances quite early on; their home, their family, their job and even whether they have a cat – these are all things that you probably need to indicate in the first few chapters. Aside from introducing and telling us a little about the character if something is important, such as the fact they have a large dog, it probably will feel a little artificial if it is only mentioned at the moment when the burglar breaks into the house. That said, the part of the novel where you establish the central character and their situation can extend quite far into the story, so don't jam all the information into a few pages. Let the information come out naturally, ideally through action and interactions. In other words, and as mentioned in an earlier chapter, show, don't tell. If you want to introduce Sybil's situation and relationships, it might be best done by showing her at home and then engaging with her friends and her son. Allowing the reader to observe Sybil and her situation and come to their own conclusions will often be the best introduction to her character.

What is their personality?

Having placed your character in your fictional world, found out about their past and established their appearance and situation, you have given the reader quite a lot of information about them and probably already given them insights into the character's personality. That doesn't mean that you shouldn't ask yourself a few more questions.

Does your central character have an internal conflict or flaw that needs to be addressed?

If so, you have a useful addition to your storytelling toolbox. If, for example they lack confidence at the beginning of the novel, it may well be they will in due course acquire the confidence they need to pursue the goal that the story sets for them. Sybil, for example, might find it difficult to open herself up to possible love, only for the story to offer her an opportunity to change that. If Wayne has allowed ambition to suppress his natural generosity of spirit, then the story may encourage him to revisit that decision. If either of them has an addiction to alcohol or drugs, then this will create practical and emotional problems that will change the course of the novel. In some novels, the internal flaw or conflict that the central character must address is the whole purpose of the story. In others, it is an added bonus to achieving the main objective.

What is their main virtue? What does your character stand for?

If your novel has a particular theme or underlying issue that you want to explore, you may want to reflect this through the central character. Let's say your central character, in a novel about the greed of the art world, is a painter who represents artistic integrity. Their determination to remain true to their artistic vision, combined with a refusal to compromise, might be what drives them. By giving your character a virtue that relates to your theme, you begin to define their role in the novel and the challenges they will face. If your artist has this pure vision of how they should approach their craft, then perhaps this will affect them financially. If it is difficult for them to obtain materials, perhaps a gallery owner will offer to help in exchange for paintings of a kind that would undermine that artistic integrity. Likewise, if your artist's determination to pursue their craft in a certain way becomes obsessive, it may cause conflict with their lover or their family. If their days are entirely taken up with painting, they may have little time for their children. Upon realising this, they may find they have to compromise.

It follows on from this that the other characters in the novel will tend to stand in opposition to the virtue or value that the central character represents – so if the artist stands for artistic integrity, an oppositional character may see art solely as a means of making money. It may also be the case that many of the challenges our central character will face over the course of the novel will be, to an extent, temptations to betray the virtue that they embody, possibly to the point where they are on the brink of abandoning their principles, which in a novel like this would be a rejection of their main virtue. In this case, the way in which they deal with that temptation would probably be a key point in the story's structure.

What motivates your central character?

Your central character may have motivations other than virtues that define them, or flaws that need to be addressed. For example, there may be something in their current situation or past that provides a strong incentive for why they feel or behave as they do. There might be loyalty or love for another character, a past evil that needs to be atoned for or a desire for freedom or success. Often the primary motivation in a novel is connected to the objective the central character will attempt to achieve at the end of the novel. For example, if the novel is focussed on the romantic relationship between the central character and another character, then the desire to be with that person will be their main motivation. Similarly, in a crime novel, a detective set the task of solving a murder will probably be motivated by a desire to discover and administer justice to the killer.

Your central character may, however, have more than one motivation and once you establish an objective-based motivation, it is worth thinking about whether you can add others that may be useful not only for the main storyline but also for sub-plots, particularly those related to sub-plots that reveal their character in some way. Sometimes it is good to include a secondary motivation that conflicts with the main motivation. For example, if Wayne's main motivation is to battle injustice, his secondary motivation may be to be successful in his career at his large law firm. If, then, the firm represents a chemical manufacturer that is poisoning a local community's water supply, Wayne may find that his career aims are inconsistent with his desire to combat injustice. This is good for the story as the conflicting motivations present a difficult decision that he will have to take one way or another.

Wayne's other motivations may be more related to sub-plots. If he cares for his younger sister who is very musically talented, then ensuring his sister achieves success in her field might be the objective of a sub-plot. The advantage of sub-plots like this, and the motivation of familial love, is that they will show an aspect of Wayne's character that may not be revealed by the main plot. They may also present the central character in a favourable light to the reader.

Once you have established what drives your central character's involvement in the story, it is worth looking at how it compares with the motivations of the other important characters in the novel. If all the characters have very similar concerns, this may be a missed opportunity for conflict. If, for example, our detective discovers their partner, who is also best friend, is attempting to cover up corruption, then that will place the detective in a difficult situation. Likewise, if your novel is about a young woman seeking to achieve success as a writer, then having parents who are opposed to this career choice is a going to make achieving success more difficult, which is good for your story. If the writer's parents are supportive while all the other characters (agents, publishers, lovers and so on) are not, then they may be a useful resource for her to call on when those other characters place obstacles in her way or undermine her ambition.

The central character's motivation may change over the course of the novel. If the personal cost of Wayne's efforts to succeed are higher than he is prepared to pay, he may change his mind. Perhaps the request from the law firm that he represent the chemical polluter will force him to go rogue and represent the local community instead. Most central characters will be changed by their story, and perhaps recovering his commitment to justice is the change that Wayne will achieve.

Does your central character have an extraordinary ability or knowledge?

Your reader may find it easier to identify with an 'ordinary' central character than someone who is completely outside the range of their experience but if your 'ordinary' central character has something extraordinary about them, although perhaps hidden to begin with, this can be pleasing from a story point of view, as well as revealing of an aspect of the central character's personality. If, for example, Sybil has a black belt in karate, that might not be something we would expect of an elderly woman. At the same time, it might allow Sybil to deal with a problem in the story that she wouldn't be able to resolve otherwise.

You can reveal Sybil's karate skills before she has to use them, which would help build her personality but the revelation might also work as a surprise, undermining the reader's previous perception of her. Sometimes the extraordinary ability, and the central character's coming to terms with it, is the whole story. If Wayne is a superb chess player, as well as a lawyer, you might show him playing a game in the first chapter and revealing how much pleasure it gives him. If Wayne becomes unhappier with his career as the story progresses, chess might turn out to be an alternative avenue of success. The story could then be about him overcoming setbacks, learning from his mistakes and displaying the toughness and mental aptitude that will allow him to make his way up the chess rankings to achieve the title of Grandmaster.

Does your central character have the capacity to surprise?

While you probably want to have a good idea of how your central character will react in any given situation, it's worth retaining enough flexibility or mystery about them that occasionally they will surprise the reader (an example would be Sybil's surprising karate skills). If the central character, or indeed the novel as a whole, is too predictable then that can affect the reader's engagement. Withholding of information about the central character is one way to achieve this. For example, the central character may proceed through most of the novel with a secret which, once revealed, will throw a very different light on their role in the story. Sybil might have a secret child with a former lover. Wayne may turn out to have been infiltrating the law firm to uncover its misdeeds. Often when there is a twist in the novel or it takes an unexpected direction, it is caused by the central character revealing themselves to be not quite what we have thought up to that point. It can also work well to make the character's personality unpredictable. If you deliberately introduce an element of mayhem into Sybil's character, for example, then she will be more interesting to the reader. Perhaps, because she is bored with her current existence, she likes to shake up both herself and the world around from time to time.

Does your central character have the capacity to change?

The central character will often be a different person at the end of the novel to the one they were at the beginning, and the change will come about because of their experiences in the story and how they have reacted to them. In order for this alteration to take place, their character needs to be capable of change. Your story will provide triggers for this transformation, perhaps in the form of opportunities or adversity but a very stable, one-dimensional character will be less capable of changing convincingly. Sometimes the change will be a prerequisite for them achieving their objective. In *Pride and Prejudice,* for example, Mr Darcy wishes to marry Elizabeth Bennet and Elizabeth Bennet wishes to marry for love. Unfortunately for Mr Darcy, she takes a dim view of his perceived arrogance. In order for the characters to achieve the goal of the novel, which is their marriage, Mr Darcy will have to become less arrogant and reveal more of his considerable (although hidden) qualities. In turn, Elizabeth will have to be a little less inflexible in order to see these qualities and appreciate them.

Revealing the central character

It is often best to introduce the central character to the reader through a series of events, conversations and encounters that show their personality and situation in a natural way that feels like part of the story. You can take your time: the reader may need to know quite a lot about the central character but they don't have to be told everything in the first chapter. If your novel is largely about the central character's profession, such as being a detective, you might want to start with them questioning a witness, or chasing a suspect. A novel about an actor might begin with them preparing to go on stage. You probably also want to indicate that they are the central character. To an extent, this will be implied by their being the focus of the opening chapters but you may also want to think about introducing the objective they will be attempting to achieve quite early in order to clarify their role. For example, in a romantic novel you will probably establish very early on that the central character is likeable and engaging and that they are romantically available.

Usually you'll want to give the central character's name when they are introduced, their sex and some indication of age, although this can often be indicated by the activity they are engaged in. A character like Sybil, for example, is more likely to be attending a t'ai chi class in the local park than a character like Wayne. Wayne, on the other hand, might skateboard to work. In some novels there may be a narrative purpose to withholding some basic information, such as the real identity of the central character in a spy novel, but otherwise it's best to get it on the page quite early on.

If you are going to give a physical description of the central character, which you may not want to, then it's best to do this early in the novel. As mentioned before, this can be quite difficult to do if you are telling the entire story from their point of view. However, you may be able to have them look at themselves in a mirror, or examine an old photograph and consider how they have changed, or even have them compare themselves to another person. In each case they are looking at a reflection of themselves (even, to an extent when they are comparing themselves to another person) but you can also reveal something about their appearance from how people react to them. If they are attractive, members of the opposite sex will flirt with them and if they are athletic, you can show that through physical action.

If you do decide to have your central character look at themselves through a reflection, then it is probably a good opportunity for the point of view character to give more than a physical description. The central character may look at themselves as a person and consider whether the attributes they want to see displayed by their facial features are there. If they would like to appear kindly to other people, they may look for how that attribute is displayed. Do they consider their face open and friendly, or is it more closed? They may also see characteristics that they would probably rather not see – such as grief, or melancholy or perhaps even anger. They will almost certainly see the passage of time, and they may see an echo of their former self which will give them an opportunity to consider how they have changed.

Some writers deliberately don't describe their central character in detail, giving just enough information for the reader to create their own image. This can mean, if it works, that the reader is working alongside you to create a visual image of the character which is personal to them, and is therefore engaged.

It is often wise to save other information about the central character until it is required by the story, although it is often sensible to foreshadow or tease very surprising information about the central character so that it's sudden revelation doesn't seem too heavy handed. Although, as mentioned before, a surprise, if properly explained afterwards, can recalibrate the reader's expectations of the central character. If a detective turns out to be an excellent jazz pianist, then it may make the reader, and the other characters, see him in a different light.

Dialogue can be a good way to give information but it can sometimes feel clunky and stilted if not handled carefully. Ideally, you always want conversations between the characters to sound natural to the ear. It would probably be less than ideal to have another character greet Sybil outside the local train station with: *'How was your holiday in Tokyo? It must be hard travelling with your artificial leg, the result of that climbing accident on Mount Everest.'* If the characters know each other well, they might discuss the holiday in Tokyo, but the rest of the information will probably have to be given in another way.

Introducing the physical and social details of the surroundings in which the novel takes place can often be a good opportunity to indicate how your character fits into them. If they are part of the landscape and the community, they will interact with their environment in one way. If they are an outsider, in another.

One possibility is to introduce the central character in the middle of a difficult situation. This will allow them to show aspects of their personality that will interest the reader, as well as kick-starting the plot. If your central character faces initial adversity or embarrassment with wit and humour, for example, this will probably make the reader warm to them. If they face danger with resourcefulness and bravery, while showing leadership and care for others then, again, we'll probably be on their side.

Can your central character carry the novel?

Because of the way that we read stories, and because we often tell them through either the close third-person or first-person point of view of the central character, it is important that they are someone in whose company the reader wants to spend time. If the reader has no point of engagement and no interest in the central character, the reader will be unlikely to give a novel the (cumulative) eight or nine hours it will take them to read it.

A dull or interesting central character is not ideal, while a character with exceptional intellectual and physical attributes, of an even and outgoing temperament and without any flaws or demons, will most likely cope easily with the challenges and obstacles the story presents to them – and that's not very useful either. For example, a kind, generous central character with no enemies is going to struggle to create the conflict with other characters that your story will require to give it momentum. The solution, then, is to give them a more complex personality, and provide them with problems and dilemmas which the story will allow them to address. If, for example, your central character is in all respects admirable, but lacks courage and self-confidence, these are self-imposed challenges which they will have to overcome. These will also probably be challenges the reader will find interesting.

Aside from making your central character complex, with some kind of weakness or flaw, you can also allow the story to transform an initially not particularly appealing character into someone more worthy of the reader's attention. For example, a shy young woman in Nazi-occupied France may discover hidden strengths that are as much of a surprise to her as they are to the reader. The extraordinary pressure and danger of the situation may turn her from an ordinary person into an extraordinary one.

Another aspect to consider is the reader's expectations of the kind of novel that you are writing. For example, if you are writing a crime novel, you may find that there are genre expectations which you wish to follow or, alternatively, subvert. If you were writing a police procedural you might wish to have a gentle, slightly timid detective instead of a hard-boiled veteran of the streets. Or you might want to have a grumpy misanthrope as the love interest in a novel with a romantic storyline. A ghost story, for example, might be better told from the perspective of someone who is sensitive and perhaps predisposed to notice the supernatural but it might also work well with someone who is dubious about the existence of spirits and anything along those lines.

Your central character doesn't have to be a nice person in order to be interesting to the reader but they will have to have some other quality that gives them appeal – for example, by being witty or intelligent. Although Hannibal Lecter isn't the central character in *Silence of the Lambs*, he is an interesting example to consider. He is malevolent and manipulative and probably not someone you would want to have around for dinner (not least because of his tendency to eat his fellow diners) but, by virtue of his intelligence and wit, he is engaging.

Have you chosen the right central character?

This might be a slightly surprising question to ask at the end of this chapter, but it is worth considering. I read a reasonable number of novels by aspiring writers every year and I am surprised by the high proportion in which it feels as though a less than ideal central character has been chosen from the available cast. One sign that the central character may not be pulling their weight is if the key decisions and events of the story happen to them, rather than as a result of their own actions. If the story is their story, they should probably be the one driving it. If, instead of them making the key decisions and being involved in the key moments of action, another character has taken on that role, ask yourself whether the decision-making character is a more worthy protagonist or ensure that the central character makes those decisions instead. If someone else is doing all the hard narrative work, in terms of overcoming challenges and obstacles and achieving the objective, think carefully about why that is the case and whether it should be changed.

When trying to understand the motivations of each of the characters in a novel, I often find it useful to remind myself that, from their perspective, *they* are the central character. By extension, it is probably sensible to consider whether one of the other characters may have a more interesting version of the story. For example, if you were planning to tell the story of a romance between a princess and a commoner, the princess would work very well as a central character but the commoner might turn out to be a more interesting alternative.

If you are satisfied that you've chosen the correct central character, make sure that the reader is aware of your choice. Sometimes, other significant characters take up too much of the story and you may need to adjust this so that they don't take away from the focus on the central character.

Summary

As a summary to this chapter, I have consolidated ten key questions to help you begin developing your central character/s.

1. What is their name/nickname? How old are they?
2. Describe them – weight, height, appearance etc.
3. Are they likeable, and if so why?
4. What is their current occupation? How did they get there? Did they do something else in the past?
5. Are they a leader or a follower? A lone wolf or a team player?
6. Do they have an internal conflict/something in their past that they will have to resolve during the story?
7. Who do they love? Spouse/lover/friend/child etc?
8. What is their main virtue?
9. What is their main fault?
10. Do they have a surprising skill, unusual knowledge or something that makes them good at what they do?

CHAPTER 5

Subsidiary characters

Your central character is the focus of your story but your novel will almost certainly need other characters as well, each of which will probably have an important role to perform. These 'subsidiary' characters are unlikely to be as important as the central character, but they will often be just as complex and developed, as well as being essential to your story. A very few novels, of course, manage to make do with no subsidiary characters but even Robinson Crusoe had Friday, a dog and a cat. Most novels, including most probably yours, need them because they force the central character to do things they wouldn't otherwise do. They also make things difficult which would otherwise be easy, and they provide motivation, emotion and conflict. Subsidiary characters do lots of other things as well, of course, but the important thing is that they make the central character engage with the story.

Why do you need *this* particular subsidiary character in your novel?

This is a question it is worth asking about every significant character in the novel, and probably the less significant ones as well. The central character is in the novel, primarily, to journey towards – and hopefully achieve – an objective. For example, in a crime novel the detective will aim to solve the crime and in a romance novel a lover will hope to enter into a lasting relationship with the object of their affections. In other novels, the central character may have to stand up to domineering parents and find their own way in life or lead a revolution to overthrow a tyrant. In each case, the bulk of the novel will be about the central character's progress towards their end goal, with the final part of the novel revolving around their success (or perhaps failure). Subsidiary characters generally justify their place in your novel because they either help or hinder that progress.

By way of explanation, if you're reading a novel at the same time as you're reading this, see if you can assign one or more of these justifications for their inclusion to each of its subsidiary characters.

They provide the central character with an objective, or they provide the character with motivation to achieve an objective.

In a love story, where Jill, our central character, falls in love with Tom, Jill's objective will be to achieve happiness with Tom. Tom's primary role in the novel therefore is to be Jill's objective. Tom will probably have other things to do apart from sitting around waiting to fall in love with Jill, but without him being loved, and coming to love Jill in return, it would be a different story. Similarly a detective in a murder mystery will be trying to catch the killer so therefore they will be the detective's main objective. If the murderer is not found, there is no murder mystery.

The victim, on the other hand, will provide motivation for the detective to achieve the objective, as well any characters affected by the victim's death. As a result, it will often be the case that the detective feels a particular connection with the victim, either because they knew them personally, or because something about the victim or the crime triggers an emotional response, or perhaps because there is a parallel with a similar murder in their past. It may be the detective's job to solve the murder but now they have an added motivation, and more emotional engagement with the investigation, and an author will be hoping that this will also mean increased engagement from the reader.

They prevent or obstruct the central character from achieving their objective.

Once you know what the central character's objective is in a novel, you will often find yourself creating a series of characters each of whose role in the novel is to make achieving the objective difficult. After all, if the objective were easily achieved your story would be both short and not very interesting. If you were writing the love story between Tom and Jill, for example, and there were no obstacles to their mutual attraction, then your story is over before it starts. However, if Jill's ex-boyfriend Mark provides competition for Tom, then things become more complicated; and if Tom's ex-girlfriend, Sarah, also attempts to rekindle her relationship with Tom, then the journey towards the objective becomes more complicated still. You might also want to add in some reluctant family members: Jill's mother might disapprove of Tom, while Tom's sister may have had an unfortunate misunderstanding with Jill in the past that has led to enmity. The lovers will have to resolve all of these complications before true love's course runs smoothly.

The usefulness of characters getting in between the central character and their objective is apparent in every kind of novel, or at least novels with plots that have beginnings, middles and ends. If we were to write a novel about an environmentalist trying to protect an area of virgin rainforest, we would probably want to create a series of characters who were committed to destroying it, as otherwise there would be no threat. We could also make use of characters who were professional or emotional rivals to our central character, or a boss who believes the environmentalist would be better deployed elsewhere. Characters don't have to be directly opposed to make the central character's life more difficult: you might create a colleague who is incompetent, if well meaning, and another character who distracts the environmentalist's attention at a key moment. Perhaps the local people who would also like to protect the rainforest distrust the activist at first. Or if our environmentalist finally manages to get local support and comes up with a plan then perhaps another colleague will disagree with the plan, delaying vital funding.

Subsidiary characters provide conflict in each of these examples. Aside from outright resistance and confrontation, if you introduce different agendas or viewpoints into any discussion or negotiation, then you have immediately made the likelihood that the central character's objective in the conversation will be harder to achieve.

Either one of the characters will get everything they want or there will have to be a compromise, generally orchestrated by the central character. Conflict with the other characters in the novel can show the central character's personality and how they react to adversity. Conflict with the other characters also often leads to tension and risk for the central character and danger or the prospect of danger (even if it's only emotional, as in the rejection of a declaration of love) is what makes readers read on.

They assist the central character in achieving their objective.
Your novel will probably also require characters who assist them in overcoming the obstacles and challenges placed in their path. If Jill's mother is not keen on Tom, then perhaps Jill's father will win her around. If Tom's sister mistakenly believes that Jill is manipulative and shallow, then you may create a mutual friend to put Tom's sister straight. There may be other characters who act as go-betweens and matchmakers and some characters may provide both obstacles and solutions. For example, the exes, Mark and Sarah, may solve the obstacle they each represent by falling in love with each other.

Characters that help overcome obstacles and challenges don't always have to want to do this. As with Sarah and Mark, the solutions they provide may be more to do with their own desires than helping the central character, and sometimes the actions they take may be intended to be an obstacle. Jill's mother, for example, may seek to put an end to the relationship by sending Jill to visit her grandmother in Paris, not realising that Tom will be there at the same time.

Much of the time, the central character will solve the problem that they face using their own resources and initiative but if a problem seems insurmountable for our central character, then it can be sensible to allow another character to help them to overcome it.

They tell us something about the central character or the setting.
Sometimes we need characters who aren't directly connected to the plot to tell us something about the central character. If Tom's

grandmother were very ill, for example, his caring for her might show Tom in a different light to the reader and, perhaps, a more positive one. How he deals with grief and sadness might show an emotional side to him that the reader won't find in other parts of the novel. If we wanted to show our environmentalist in a different light, we could give him a child, or a younger sibling. Other characters might exist to tell us about the central character's history or background or to allow the central character to be humorous or to display bravery. These other characters may have little role in the main plot (in which the central character aims to achieve their objective) but they may be part of a sub-plot (for more on sub-plot, see Chapter 6). Sub-plots often relate back to the main plot but sometimes they exist completely separately and solely to show the character in a different light.

Some characters exist only to provide information about the setting. Particularly at the beginning of a novel, you may need a character to show the central character (and the reader) around. This character can explain the local situation to the extent it is relevant, introduce other characters that are going to play important roles and warn of dangers or risks. For example, in my novel *The Constant Soldier*, the central character, disabled and disfigured by injury, returns to the Silesian valley in which he grew up before World War II. A female station master exists to explain how the valley has changed since it became part of Nazi Germany, and to give an indication of how he will fit into the changed environment.

If a subsidiary character's inclusion isn't justified by one of these four reasons, it doesn't mean that you shouldn't include them but it *does* mean you should look objectively at their role in the novel and consider whether it should be adjusted. Also, bear in mind that some characters will be included for more than one reason. For example, Jill's father may initially disapprove of Tom and do his best to prevent Tom seeing her but, won over by Tom's charm, he may change his mind and try to help the couple find happiness. It could also be the case that her father, through his actions and dialogue, will tell the reader, and perhaps Tom, about Jill's personality and childhood. Jill's father could even provide her with motivation by telling her about how he and Jill's mother had to struggle to convince their own parents that they were a suitable match.

Who are they?

If you've reassured yourself that a character has earned their place in your novel then it's probably time to find out a little bit more about them. Developing your subsidiary character's appearance, back story, situation and personality will follow very closely the methods used to develop and refine a central character. However, there are some elements that are specific to the role of a subsidiary character, and some questions that can be usefully asked of them with a view to discovering unexpected information that may help your story.

Who do they appear to be and who are they really?

Not every character will have a secret past or a hidden agenda, but it is something you should consider for each of them. With some characters, the hidden element you come up with may be very significant. If Tom's best friend and confidante, Ted, were to secretly be in love with Jill, for example, you can imagine how this might significantly change the story. With other characters, knowing what they keep hidden may give an added dimension to their behaviour or relationships. By hiding something about a character, but hinting at the existence of a secret, you make them intriguing and potentially surprising to the reader. Your knowledge of the hidden element, and the knowledge that you'll be revealing it later on, will also shape how you draw the character and how the character behaves. Your reader will, consciously or subconsciously, pick up on your preparations and will be more interested in, and intrigued by, your character as a result. In addition, you are creating a (largely) unexpected development later in the novel.

What is their objective over the course of the novel and what motivates them?

As you develop the characters in your novel, the likelihood is that they will become more and more real, at least in your mind (this is particularly true of the central character). However, while the subsidiary characters have subordinate roles, that doesn't mean that it isn't worth knowing what they are trying to achieve and why. After all, as far as subsidiary characters in your novel are concerned, their motivations and aspirations are of primary importance. Just as the actual central character's role in the story involves overcoming obstacles and challenges to achieve an objective, then each of the subsidiary characters will have their own objective to achieve, and challenges and obstacles to face. Looking at the novel from their perspective not only helps your plot, but can also help you to understand and develop the subsidiary character.

For example, if Tom's objective is to win Jill's heart, a good plot will require other characters intent on preventing him being successful. In other words, once we establish what Tom wants, we should create other characters with objectives and intentions that oppose Tom as these will translate into obstacles. Ted, Tom's lovelorn best friend, is in love with Jill and therefore motivated to make Tom's journey towards his objective more difficult. Similarly, Tom may feel guilty about his burgeoning relationship with Jill because he knows it will hurt his best friend. As a result, he may be more cautious about revealing his emotions to Jill or, if he does reveal them, more reticent about following through on them. Ted may also take a more active role in the novel, either by misleading Tom about Jill's feelings towards him or, perhaps, misleading Jill about Tom's feelings. Ted may also be very attractive and eligible, perhaps more so than Tom, which will force Tom to find ways to compensate and make Jill's decision to fall in love with him less obvious. If Ted and Jill are already in a long-standing if unstable relationship, Tom's task will become more difficult still. At the same time, we can be asking interesting questions of Ted: why does he love Jill and are his motivations entirely romantic? Is he prepared to sacrifice his friendship with Tom in order to pursue his relationship with Jill? Is his relationship with Tom complicated by hidden emotions, such as jealousy or anger? By considering Ted's conflicting motivations of wanting to be a friend to Tom and a lover to Jill, we give Ted a moral dilemma that may make him a more complex and interesting character than he would have been otherwise.

Not all subsidiary characters' objectives and motivations need to be in direct opposition to those of the central character in order to change the direction of the story. For example, Tom's sister may attempt to act as a matchmaker and this may go well...or very badly. Her intentions may be good, but her execution may lead to a misunderstanding that needs to be overcome. Alternatively, she may not like Jill and therefore do her best to prevent the couple getting together. Her efforts, again, may produce unintended consequences.

Once you start asking what motivates a subsidiary character and what they hope to achieve at the end of the novel, possibilities present themselves that can influence the story and shape the character, perhaps by making them more complex, or sympathetic, or antagonistic. If you understand why a character behaves a certain way, remember to have the subsidiary character reveal their motivations to the reader. If the reader doesn't understand their motivation, the subsidiary character's actions may not be credible.

It is also worth bearing in mind that the subsidiary characters do not need to be consistent in their motivation. Their motivation may change over the course of the novel and be shaped by the actions of the other characters and the events that unfold.

Aside from motivation, what else will influence a character's behaviour?

While it's always good to know a subsidiary character's motivations and personal objectives, it's probably also the case that they won't explain all of their behaviour. They will have other desires, inclinations and character attributes that will lead them towards certain actions. If, for example, they are scared of the dark, they'll be reluctant to enter an abandoned house at night. Likewise, if they are brave and a bit foolhardy, then this may be enough for them to help a stranger who is being attacked, even if the action is tangential to their personal objective. Once you know that a character has to do something not directly connected to their central motivation, consider whether there are elements of their personality, backstory or emotional state – or some other reason – that will allow them to take the course of action that you'd like them to.

Do they have a hidden link to the objective?

When developing the other characters in the novel, it's worth considering whether they have a secret connection to the objective and how it might explain their wider role in the novel. If a character's link to the objective is revealed at the outset, it provides them with straightforward motivation as well as suggesting their relationship with the central character. If the connection to the objective is hidden, its revelation may well be a key moment in the novel, placing everything that has happened in the novel up to that point in a new light. A hidden connection of this kind is relatively common in genre fiction, particularly crime and romance, but is found in all kinds of novels. But beware: while a hidden connection can provide a new aspect to your story it can also, if not handled carefully, appear a little contrived.

For example, if a character in a crime novel is the unanticipated heir of a murder victim, that may make them a suspect and, when it is revealed, cause a significant change in the direction of the story. If the character is innocent of the crime, the revelation of the inheritance will be a distraction to the investigation which will affect the identification the real killer. On the other hand, if the character is responsible for the murder, not only will the revelation of the inheritance be a key step forward for the investigation, but that character will probably have been attempting to mislead the investigation prior to that point. If the character is unaware that they are due to inherit, then the inheritance is unlikely to be a motive for the crime, but that doesn't mean that they are innocent of the murder. In this case, the revelation of the victim's generosity to their murderer may be a nice twist. If the heir isn't aware of their inheritance, it doesn't mean that the inheritance might not be a motive for murder for another character who has been passed over.

Do they have a hidden link to the central character?

A hidden link to the central character (as opposed to their objective) can enhance a subsidiary character's role in the main story, provide a useful storyline separate to the main plot or make the subsidiary character's relationship with the protagonist more complex. Hidden links often revolve around relationships such as hidden romantic or familial connections. It is surprising, in the latter case, how often the central character turns out to have secret blood relationships with other characters in the novel. While hidden romantic interests are also common, the opposite may also be true: a subsidiary character might hold a longstanding resentment or even hatred towards the central character which will provide strong motivation over the course of the novel, generally to the central character's disadvantage.

Do they tell always the truth?

The central character's journey to the end of the novel often relies on information from the other characters. In addition, the central character's motivations, behaviour and actions, as well as those of the other characters in the novel, are often decided by what they believe to be true. Your subsidiary characters will probably tell the truth most of the time but, occasionally, it is useful for your story if they don't. Considering if and when each of your characters might not want to tell the truth is a question which, when asked, may reveal that your subsidiary character is more complex than you previously thought and, depending on the lies they tell, suggest ways in which they can complicate your story (in a good way). The practical effects of a deception may include misunderstandings, misdirection, characters being in conflict who wouldn't otherwise be and changes to the direction of the story. In addition, being deceived or misled can make the central character's journey towards their objective much more complicated than it would be otherwise. If Tom is misled into thinking that Jill is in love with Ted, then that is a misunderstanding which is going to delay Tom and Jill realising their mutual attraction, and possibly lead to a series of other misunderstandings as well. Similarly, if your novel were about a fractured relationship between a father and son, then a misunderstanding, created by the mother, about the father's past behaviour might be at the heart of the estrangement.

A character may mislead because they want to intentionally deceive, or because they are mistaken or because they feel forced to do so. For example, if a witness in a crime novel lies to a detective about what they saw on the night of the murder, they may be seeking to protect themselves, or to protect a loved one, or to keep an embarrassing secret, or any number of other reasons. They could be acting maliciously – to direct suspicion towards a character they have an aversion to – or they honestly believe that character is responsible for the crime. Indeed they might have more than one reason for misleading the detective, and when those reasons are in opposition to each other, their motivation could be even more complex.

In fiction, as in real life, characters will also sometimes seek to withhold or distort information in order to avoid causing hurt or offence or to save themselves from embarrassment. If a soldier has to tell the mother of a dead comrade how he died, he may see little point in describing the pain and terror of her son's last moments. The fact of his death remains the same, but the soldier's kindness and tact in glossing over the details may show them in a positive light to one of the other characters (and to the reader).

Do they behave logically?

It is nearly always sensible if events in your novel have a logical flow from one to the next. Similarly, it is advisable that your characters react to the events of the story in predictable ways. Asking yourself whether your character is behaving logically in a particular situation isn't going to tell you anything new about them, but it may help you spot inconsistencies in their behaviour which would be equally visible to a reader. Sometimes, as writers, we create a series of events and place our characters in them without necessarily thinking too much about their behaviour. Characters can, of course, behave in unexpected ways but if the behaviour is confusing to the reader, it needs to be explained. If, for example, a shy and retiring stamp collector suddenly turns into an action hero, it will be more credible if we have established the necessary motivation and physical attributes. For example, if we show them exercising against a tae kwon-do black belt in an early chapter, and show them standing up to in intimidating drunk at another point, then we will have prepared the reader for the new development. Almost any kind of behaviour or action by a character can be justified if we do the groundwork to establish its credibility.

Aside from foreshadowing unexpected behaviour, it is also worth considering a character's reactions to an event. If someone close to them dies, do they grieve? If they are hurt, do they feel pain? If someone says something that insults them, do they react? As you develop your characters, remember to allow them to have natural emotional and practical responses to events in which they are a participant, even if they aren't the focus of attention in a particular scene.

If they are attracted (or otherwise) to another character, have you explained why?

This question is one to bear in mind when taking an overview of your story and the character interactions. Relationships' credibility (or rather lack thereof) is a common complaint from readers, particularly when it comes to romantic relationships. If you, as the writer, haven't established attraction and shared desire between the characters in your own mind, then the relationship is unlikely to be convincing to the reader. It's often worth listing the points of attraction. If the lovers find each other physically attractive, that's probably a good starting point. If one of them values a virtue that the other possesses, such as altruism, so much the better. The lovers may also have shared interests, experiences, or concerns which may help them bond as they move through the story. Most importantly, however, they must have an emotional connection that is clear to the reader. The reasons can be unusual – even absurd – but if they are consistent with the characters' personality and desires, and are explained, the reader will probably find them believable. What they may not accept, however, are unlikely attractions that are then not explained at all – or, at least, not adequately.

There is generally more flexibility when it comes to familial relationships, as families are often more tolerant of idiosyncrasies and behavioural oddities that others find difficult. Similarly, some friendships could be based around longstanding connections that are no longer as clear as they once were. Childhood friends, for example, can have very close bonds that have survived considerable changes in situation and personality, but it might be useful to clarify the original basis of the relationship to the reader.

Antipathies have similar requirements when it comes to to the reader. If one character despises another, the contrast in personality, behaviour and situation may indicate immediately why this is the case. Where the antipathy is less clear, however, another character could explain it, either through their internal thoughts or in dialogue. Dislikes do not always have to be rational – and the antagonism may often say more about the character than the person they hate – but you need to understand why the relationship is toxic in order to explain it to the reader.

Does a relationship between important characters change over the course of the novel?

Fictional relationships (as in real life) are not static and may well change over the course of your novel. Enemies will become friends and characters that aren't attracted to each other will suddenly find themselves hopelessly in love, while happily married couples will end up divorced. It's often useful to look at the important characters in the novel, and particularly the central character, then consider how their relationships may change and how this might help the story. Often, as mentioned previously, a subsidiary character's role is to either hinder or help the central character in their journey towards their objective. If we think of the subsidiary characters in terms of the central character's objective, is it possible that a change in their relationship with the central character will have an influence, whether positive or negative, on their progress towards that goal?

Do they create conflict for the central character?

Conflict between your central character and your subsidiary character doesn't have to be based on a clash of personalities. Differing motivations, contrasting perspectives and many other reasons can lead to differences of opinions that will have to be worked through. Conflict in these terms doesn't necessarily mean confrontation. For example, the characters could take opposing, but amicable, positions on the way to approach a problem. Often these discussions will reach a compromise or will persuade the central character into proceeding in a different way. These discussions will, of course, be much more vigorous when you add in antipathy and/or conflicting motivations. It's important that the subsidiary characters conflict with the central character because it will make the protagonist's journey to their objective more difficult, as well as telling the reader something about the personality of the characters involved. For example, Jill and Tom want to go on a date but he wants to have dinner in a restaurant while she wants to see a band play in a bar. Even though it's a small decision, there will have to be a discussion and one or both of them will have to show flexibility. It may sound unimportant, but that flexibility might be key to the development of their relationship.

Conflict works very well to complicate the central character's progress through the novel and, as conflict often comes via interactions with the subsidiary characters, you should constantly be looking for opportunities to create it. Whenever the central character is engaging with another character, there is the opportunity for that character to question or challenge the central character in some way.

Each subsidiary character will probably create different kinds of conflict for the central character. If the conflict arises from opposed motivations with regard to the objective, then it will probably continue until the objective is achieved or the motivations are aligned. That doesn't mean that the discord will be either constant or consistent. If Tom is unaware that his best friend Ted is secretly in love with Jill, Ted may seek to prevent Tom's relationship with Jill succeeding in various ways. If Tom tells Ted he wants to go to the movies with Jill, Ted may try to persuade him this isn't a good idea. If they meet Jill in the street, Ted may try to indicate that Tom is not available. If their conflicting motivations are not visible to Tom, it makes sense that Ted's actions will be of a more devious nature. When his behaviour becomes obvious to Tom, then the conflict will be more open. They may also find conflict in completely unrelated matters, such as if they run a business together, how to expand it. However, they may also join together to face a common threat.

Other conflicts will be more about differing personalities. The relationship between Tom and his father, for example, may be based around the father being very cautious and concerned about his son's emotional and physical safety whereas Tom is somewhat rash. Or the conflict could arise from differing beliefs or prejudices. Tom's father could be a strict Roman Catholic, whereas Tom is not, or the father may not like Jill because of her ethnicity. Tom and his father may be at odds about lots of other issues, from whether he has been to see his grandmother to what will happen if he fails his university finals.

The relationships between the central character and the other characters in your novel will have their own trajectory. Sometimes, these will lead to a resolution of the conflict, either because the central character overcomes the other character's efforts to prevent them reaching their objective – in other words, they are victorious – or because the conflict-based relationship changes to one which is more supportive or collaborative. For example, Jill's grandmother (let's call her Daisy) could be unpleasant to Tom when they meet, uncertain that he is a suitable match for her granddaughter. This relationship will have to change in order for Jill and Tom's relationship to proceed. Tom will have to reveal his qualities to Daisy and she will have to be open to changing her mind about him. In this scenario, Daisy is an obstacle that has to be overcome and, in doing so, Tom may reveal positive aspects of his character. However, Daisy might dislike Tom because of her previous relationship with Tom's grandfather, Bob, did not treat her well, at least in Daisy's eyes. This background could lead to a sub-plot, with Tom and Jill uncovering information which changes Daisy's understanding of that relationship, placing Bob in a much more favourable light. In this case, it is Daisy and Bob's poor relationship, and the resulting dislike of Tom, that represents the obstacle to the objective of the main plot – but it can also stand on its own as a separate story within the novel.

Managing characters

Whether you decide all the information about your characters and their situations in advance or acquire it as you go along, keep track of the decisions that you make. If nothing else, it makes it easier for you to ensure that a character's hair colour doesn't change from chapter to chapter and that events from their past are consistent. Having the information about your characters in one place as you write is of immediate practical use as a reference tool, but is also very helpful when considering your character in terms of your story. The more time you spend thinking about a character and the more you know about them, the more real they'll be in your imagination and, as a result, in the pages of your novel. If you note down your thoughts about them as you go along, you'll find that this will also help, even if much of what you know about the character doesn't make it into the pages of your manuscript. It's a bit like the background research you do for a novel, much of the knowledge you acquire about a character forms the foundation that gives your portrayal of them a feeling of authenticity, even if that foundation isn't visible. Because you know a lot about them, they acquire solidity in your mind, which allows you, all being well, to make them more visible to the reader. That having been said, you may not have to do much thinking about the minor characters. A taxi driver who follows a suspect at the detective's request isn't going to have enough time allocated to them in the novel to allow for much more than the briefest of sketches. For all the significant characters it's worth keeping note of at least the following details:

- **Physical description.** Keeping a separate note of basic information about each character, such as their age, hair colour and style, weight, height, style of dress and any other visual elements is sensible. I also find it very useful to have a photograph on which to base the character and to cut and paste it into the reference document for that character. For example, I used a black-and-white photograph taken by Aleksandr Rodchenko of a 1930s Soviet actor for a character in my novel *The Holy Thief*. The photograph seemed to represent the kind of personality I wanted the character to have but I made mental adjustments to his weight and hair, and added a sabre scar.
- **Backstory and situation.** I also want to track and keep a record of more general information about the past and present situations of the important characters. When looking at the backstory of a character, I often find it useful to present this as a timeline from birth. This allows me to have a good overview of their past, even if it contains information that doesn't make it into the novel itself.
- **Dialogue style.** If possible, consider ways in which you can differentiate how your characters speak. Often their way of

speaking comes from the character's personality, but regional accents, repeated phrases and mannerisms are all things which help make characters stand apart. In addition, characters with particular professions may use technical language and phrasing. Social class, education and even political and religious inclination will also help differentiate the characters. Having a defined voice is particularly important for POV characters, as their storytelling will use that voice.

- **Plot points.** It is useful to make notes about each character's planned role in the novel, particularly if they will reveal certain information or take a particular action. I have a chapter-by-chapter breakdown which will notes when a particular character appears and what they do. Knowing their plot functions helps me to keep track of their usefulness and how often they appear.

Although there are no absolute rules about the number of secondary characters, remember that a reader may struggle if there are too many, particularly if they are very similar. Obviously each novel is different – some, by their very nature, will be more heavily populated than others – and it's generally wise to avoid extended casts, especially when some characters' roles in the story might be easily combined.

Summary

I have created a short questionnaire providing prompts that you can use to develop your supporting cast of characters.

1. What is it about them that means they have to be involved in the story (looking beyond the obvious)?
2. Is there something about this character/these characters that allows the protagonist to show strengths, weaknesses or other important characteristics?
3. What is their relationship/conflict with the protagonist over the course of the novel? Is there a trajectory?
4. Do they have a particular motivation for their actions over the course of the novel?
5. Are they honest? With themselves? With the protagonist?
6. Who do they appear to be? Who are they *really*?

CHAPTER 6

Plot

Plotting does not mean that all decisions regarding structure, theme, setting and genre need to be made in advance or, if you do make them in advance, that they need to be rigidly adhered to. Each author will have their own approach to writing a novel. Some novelists have very detailed plans, with chapter breakdowns written in advance as well as outlines for each character and the key plot points in the novel identified and scheduled. Others have very little planned and take each chapter as it comes. I personally like to have a good idea when I sit down to begin a novel of what I want it to look like when I have finished. I will always know the ending, most of the key events and have a good sense of the main characters and how I want them to interact. I know, however, that many of these elements will develop during the writing process and that my 'plan' is more of a general direction than a rigid framework. I am, after all, always looking to improve my novel and if I have an idea for a character or event that I think will work better, then I am nearly always going to take advantage of the improvement.

It is difficult to begin plotting your story without knowing your characters or understanding the world they inhabit, so we will begin this chapter by looking at the dramatic worlds. This is something you will want to consider early in your novel planning process as it will indicate ways in which to place your characters in conflict as well as identify their motivations over the course of the book. It will often also help you clarify the central character's objective, as well as positioning the characters either in opposition to that objective, or in support.

Dramatic world

A dramatic world, in storytelling terms, is something that links the important characters and confines the story in some way. It can be something that imposes a physical restriction on the characters and the story – for example, a novel set entirely on a small island with only intermittent contact with the outside world. Alternatively, it could be a shared purpose or connection – a legal drama might have an ongoing litigation as its dramatic world, while a novel set on the American plains in the 1870s might revolve around a cattle drive or a posse hunting down a gang of desperadoes. In each case, the dramatic world provides boundaries to the story. If a character is not present on the island, then they are unlikely to be part of the main story. If a character is not involved in the litigation in some way, either as one of the parties, a witness, a lawyer or someone affected by the outcome, then they will probably have no obvious part in the main storyline of the novel. However, that doesn't mean that they won't be part of a sub-plot that is important to the novel as a whole and which might have its own dramatic world. For example, a crime novel where a detective is investigating a murder that has taken place in a hospital might have one dramatic world connected to the hospital and medicine, and another within the investigating police team. The hospital dramatic world may have a greater importance to the main storyline, but the police dramatic world might contain an interesting sub-plot. This sub-plot might revolve around corruption, and its relevance to the main story could be that the internal politics of the police team will make the detective's job more difficult.

A shared interest in a dramatic world does not mean that the characters have shared motivations; while there is a common connection to the dramatic world, the likelihood is that each of the characters will have different interests in it, and agendas. To refer back to the hospital dramatic world introduced previously, you might have a management team that wants to make changes which may cut costs but will affect the quality of patient care. There may also be a senior doctor who wants to protect his reputation and that of the hospital but is aware of mistakes that have had serious consequences for the health of a patient. Other players within this world may include a medical professional who is ending the lives of terminally ill patients without their consent or a researcher who has taken the credit for the ground-breaking research of a colleague. It is then relatively straightforward to create other characters who have opposing interests, such as the colleague whose research has been stolen and a nurse who has become suspicious of the unusual number of premature fatalities amongst those terminally ill patients. Sometimes these sub-plots will overlap, and the important characters will be in conflict, in different ways, with a number of the other characters. As this exemplar novel concerns a murder, it is likely the victim (always a pivotal character in a crime novel, even if they don't appear much on the page) will have had a series of conflicts with other characters, each of which could have provided a motive for their murder.

Identifying how the characters' differing interests in a dramatic world can create conflict is not limited to a hospital-set murder mystery. If your novel were about a family, the story might focus on the relationship between a mother and her daughter. If the relationship between the two is strained, then the mother's objective, as the central character, might be first to understand what is wrong with it and secondly, how to fix it. The mother's motivation for achieving her objective is to keep the family healthy and happy, which requires her to exert control, generally benevolent, which is nonetheless chafing for both her children and her husband. Let's say, though, that her husband is not as committed to the family as he once was – perhaps he is having an affair or he has simply had enough of family life. By leaving most of the difficult parenting to the mother, he has caused tension in the marriage, but also tension between the mother and the children to his own unearned benefit. The daughter could be aware of his affair or that he is drifting away but she chooses to unreasonably blame her mother rather than him for the situation. She may also be keen to achieve independence from her mother's restrictions and make her own way in the world. If there is another daughter and she's more on the mother's side, you can fold in some sibling rivalry. If the parents are, ostensibly, very religious and conservative and expect their family to be the same, then you can imagine that the children may find themselves in opposition to this in various ways. If the daughter is committed to various liberal causes, this may place her at odds with parents who hold traditional and conservative ideals. If she becomes pregnant, the family's varying attitudes to abortion could be brought into focus but it may also lead to a secret being revealed, perhaps that the father's girlfriend has had an abortion or, as a result of medical tests she has to take, that her father is not her biological father. The family, and their relationships, will probably be very different at the end of the novel than they were at the beginning and there may be other factors which apply still greater pressure on them as a unit – such as the mother's being diagnosed with cancer or the father's losing his well-paid job. If the secret of the daughter's parentage comes to light towards the end of the novel, this could be a catalyst for the final transformation of their relationships.

Another factor to consider when looking at a dramatic world is whether they have codes or accepted ways of behaving that the characters, at least on the surface, adhere to. The code of a dramatic world may not always be that of the wider world. The code of a crime family such as the Sopranos in the TV show of the same name may have many ways of behaving that we recognise – such as loyalty, respect and honour – but they have been perverted by the gang's overriding dedication to crime. In our hospital crime novel, we might expect a general commitment to improving the health of the patients and there will be a series of rules that have been encoded in order to ensure that general commitment is achieved. Other rules may apply, of course, such as supporting your colleagues, not betraying confidences and a prohibition on criminality. In our family drama, the members may expect mutual love, honesty, respect, adherence to certain beliefs, and a commitment to its general wellbeing and standing in their community. Once you have established the codes and ways of behaving that apply to a dramatic world, think about whether everyone should be complying with them. Are the appearance of the dramatic world and the reality at odds? If our crime family relies for its existence on a dedication to criminality and rigid loyalty, perhaps it becomes clear over the course of the novel that someone is not playing by the rules, either by working with another gang or giving information to the police. The crime family is no longer functioning as it should and, in their parallel morality, their dramatic world has been corrupted. When our detective starts investigating the murder at the hospital, it may give all the appearance of being a normal, well-functioning healthcare establishment committed to the welfare of its patients with a collegial and efficient team working towards the same aim. Over the course of the novel, though, it will probably become apparent that this is far from the truth. In this situation, the detective will act as a sort of redeemer, fixing the dramatic world as he goes along by exposing the characters who are not playing by the rules, or perhaps by changing their behaviour. In the mother and daughter family, the mother may realise that all is not as it seems with her marriage and her children. In order to fix the family, she may have to change her own behaviour by accepting her children as they are as well as perhaps addressing the flaws in her marriage, either by ending it or changing it. The outcome for the crime family, however, will depend on who the main character is and what their role is. For example, if the central character is a junior member of the family determined to end his involvement in criminality, then he could fix the corrupted world by putting its members behind bars. If the central character is the head of the crime family, however, their way of fixing the dramatic world could be to have the informer dealt with in some unsavoury way.

Before we move onto plotting a three-act structure for your novel, consolidate the ideas of developing dramatic worlds by answering the following questions:

1. What dramatic 'world' links the characters?
2. If it's a physically contained world, define its parameters.
3. If it's a 'virtual' world, what are its boundaries/what holds people within it?
4. Does the dramatic world have a code or set of principles by which it operates? Broadly speaking, what are they?
5. Is the dramatic world corrupted? How?

Three-act structure

Dramatic stories generally fall naturally into three acts, as in they have a beginning, a middle and an end. The main storyline will often follow a central character as they journey towards a defined goal, although sometimes there will be more than one central character. My novel *A House of Ghosts* follows a romantically inclined pair of spies, while other novels follow a group of characters, with famed examples being a group of sleuthing children in *The Famous Five* and the fellowship in *The Lord of the Rings* (even though it is a trilogy) which comprises a collection of individuals engaged in a common endeavour. Often the acts relate to stages of character progression as well as the story's progression: in other words, your story will change the central character in some way, perhaps giving them confidence that they didn't have before or addressing flaws in their personality or behaviour. This isn't always the case with groups of characters. For example, there isn't much personality development in *The Famous Five* once the characters are established but the characters in *The Lord of the Rings* are all profoundly altered by their experiences.

Very roughly, a three-act structure looks a little like this:

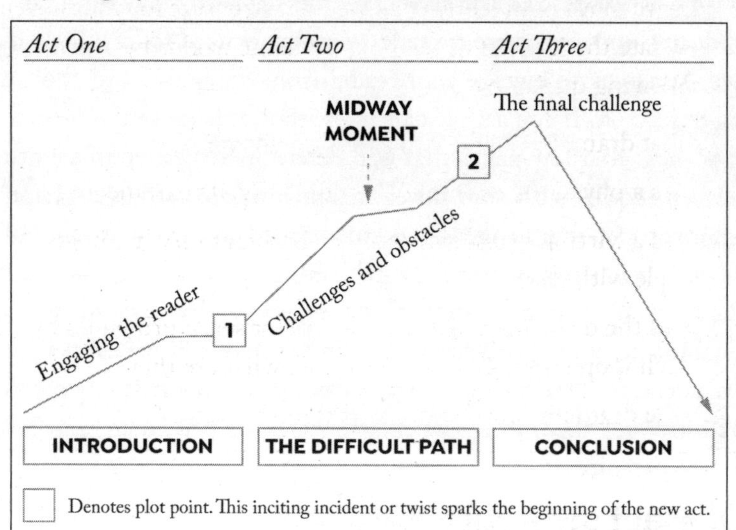

Three-act structure

As you can see, the first act is a little quieter than the following two as this is where we establish the dramatic world or worlds in which the novel takes place, introduce the important characters and the objective, and start the story in earnest. After this point, the action in the story escalates gradually until it reaches a peak in act three.

It probably makes sense to demonstrate how a plot works by creating a hypothetical novel. The story I've chosen is that of a Polish pilot who makes his way to London in World War II, where he becomes a senior fighter pilot and falls in love with two women, with varying success. As I type this, I'm not sure how it ends or what will happen in the story but it has plenty of potential for excitement and personality development so I'm sure we'll come up with something interesting.

First chapters and prologues

Before we discuss the first act in more detail, I'd like to quickly mention first chapters and prologues. While the first act generally lacks the intensity of the rest of the novel, the opening chapters – where you introduce your novel to your reader – probably need to be a little more active. You need to engage your reader from the outset and encourage them to read on. If you are an aspiring author, this is even more crucial, as it is these first few pages that will determine whether an agent or a publisher persists with your novel or puts it to one side (see Chapter 9 for more on pitching to agents). As mentioned above, the first act often involves introducing characters, establishing the setting, giving an idea of the motivations and conflicts that are going to drive the story as well as establishing an objective that the central character needs to achieve. If you spend too much time on these elements in the first few pages, or don't introduce them in a particularly engaging way, then your reader may lose patience.

The obvious place to start your novel is at the beginning of your story's timeline, so our first chapter could feature the future pilot, Jan, as a university student in Warsaw when the Germans invade Poland in September 1939. If the novel starts with the Luftwaffe bombing the city, the air raid would provide him with strong motivation to become a pilot as well as being an exciting and engaging opening. However, you don't always have to start at the chronological beginning of your story. Fiction allows us to play around with the sequence of storytelling and first chapters can be placed at the beginning, the middle or the end of the main story's timeline – as well as long before the main story starts, and long after it ends. The start may even come from a parallel storyline, or sub-plot. What is key is that those opening pages have something happening in them that hooks the reader's attention. For example, you could begin with the moment when a very young Jan sees a plane for the first time (long before the main story begins) or at his funeral in 1972 (long after the main story). One thing you are often trying to do with opening chapters is to create questions in the reader's mind that can only be answered by their reading on. One option is to start with a dramatic and unusual scene from the end of the story's timeline, then the reader will be more interested in the world-building and character development that happens in the first act because they will be looking for clues as to how the unusual and dramatic event with which the novel started came to take place. With this in mind, Jan's story could begin in late 1944 with him being dragged into the woods to be shot by the SS after his plane has crashed in enemy territory. As he is pulled along, he could contemplate the events that have led him to this time and place, before moving the story back to his university days in Warsaw. At the end of the novel we could either have him escape his execution – or not.

We could also do the same with a dramatic event from elsewhere in the timeline. If we began with a scene from the middle of the story where Jan is in a dogfight over the English channel with two German Messerschmitt 109s on his tail, then the questions we pose for the reader could be: how did Jan get to this point and will he escape being shot down?

In all of these examples, we have hopefully engaged the reader but also introduced our central character in an effective way – either through him doing something or by being remembered by the large numbers of family and friends at his funeral. It's always worth looking for a dramatic scene for the opening rather than something more mundane such as Jan meeting a friend for a drink. We could still have them catching up, which may give the reader essential information about Jan and the other character, but if this is preceded by a more memorable scene, the quieter episode will probably have an edge and interest for the reader that we would struggle to give it otherwise, no matter how well we write it.

It isn't essential to have the central character present in the very first scene of a novel but, if they aren't, they probably should arrive soon afterwards. Likewise, they don't have to be introduced in a hugely dramatic scene (although it helps). A common way to introduce the central character is by having them interacting with another character. In this kind of scene you can reveal the central character's personality through their behaviour and their reactions to whatever is happening around them (as opposed to introducing the central character through description and backstory alone). If, for example, we started with several pages about Jan's childhood, appearance and a summary of his personality, we would run the risk of boring the reader – after all, Jan means nothing to them at this stage of the novel. An interaction with another character will generally tell the reader about the central character in a more effective and engaging way.

It's also an option that the scene you choose to introduce the central character doesn't have to be part of the main story. We could meet Jan as he struggles with a motorcycle engine, say, or climbs a mountain or goes on a disastrous date. The purpose of the scene in which we meet the central character for the first time is to introduce them. Telling us something about the story at the same time is often useful, but it is not essential. Engaging the reader is our key aim here. If our scene shows Jan under pressure but reacting in a way that suggests he is someone in whose company the reader will be happy spending the next 350 pages, then it will have achieved its aim.

You may also want to use opening chapters to introduce the setting and the atmosphere (see Chapter 3), particularly if they are key elements of the novel. If your novel is contemporary, set in a place familiar to the majority of your readership and without a very defined atmosphere, you may not need to spend much time doing this. If, on the other hand, it is set in a place or a time that is unfamiliar and which needs explanation, such as Warsaw in 1939 or London in 1940, then it is wise to do this from the outset. It would be unusual, for example, if the first indication that novel is set in World War II doesn't come until the tenth page. If the world your novel is set in is a very complex one, as in a fantasy or science fiction novel, then the earlier you start explaining the way that the world works to the reader, the better. With complex and unfamiliar worlds, there is often a temptation to 'tell' how the world works, but it is always best to 'show' the world through a character's interacting with it and keep the explanation to a minimum. If we wanted to introduce Warsaw in 1939, it would be best to have Jan going about his business within the city, rather than trying to explain the situation directly through exposition.

As with setting, if the atmosphere is a key element of your novel then the earlier you establish it, the better. A novel set in a dystopian future will need to have a very specific atmosphere created through, perhaps, a sense of foreboding from the outset. Likewise, if you are writing a ghost story, you might want to begin to introduce the atmosphere that goes with it from an early stage. Jan's novel, however, is set against the background of World War II and its atmosphere will reflect that. If we were to start the novel in Warsaw, we might want to show panic in the streets, smoke from burning buildings in the distance, air-raid sirens, columns of refugees and retreating soldiers. If Jan were to appear in the novel with these elements as a background, the reader would quickly get a sense of a place gripped by fear of the approaching German army and the desperation of the inhabitants to leave.

One final element to bear in mind when approaching those opening scenes is that they should introduce you as a writer. Make sure they showcase the very best of your talent as a writer of words while also providing the reader with a clear indication of your abilities as a storyteller. Your prose has to be as good as you can make it (without veering into over-writing). At the same time, you want to give the reader a strong sense of anticipation for the story they are about to encounter.

Think of the first chapters as a hook and the reader as the fish. How are you going to reel them in?

Act one: the beginning

While the opening scene may be about grabbing the attention of the reader, the rest of the first act is mainly about setting down the foundations of your story. You may, of course, have done some of this in the opening chapter but there will certainly be more work to do. So what questions should you be asking yourself when thinking about what you need to achieve in the beginning of your story?

Have you introduced all of the important characters and established their personalities?

It is generally a good idea if all of the important characters have made an appearance by the time you move on to the middle of the novel (the second act), particularly where novels are set in one place, or within a relatively limited time frame, or revolve around a set group of people (or all three). If your story involves a journey from one place to another, with many stops and interactions along the way, or has a diverse set of characters, then introducing all the characters early may not be possible or necessary – and some novels, such as those with timelines over many years, have structures that allow important characters to enter late. That said, be wary of the overly-convenient late introduction of a character whose arrival appears designed mainly to give the plot an extra impetus or solve a structural problem. For example, if a twin brother suddenly appears in the last few pages to fill in some plot holes, readers may be suspicious. If characters aren't present initially, then it's a good idea to foreshadow their arrival, if possible, as this creates anticipation (and their late appearance will seem less jarring).

If we look at Jan's novel, the characters that surround him are likely to change over the course of the novel as he journeys from Warsaw to London and then, because of his service, moves around Britain and possibly to other parts of Europe or North Africa. It will still be sensible to give him a core group of colleagues and friends, even if not all of them survive the novel. This will be easier if he remains part of the same fighter squadron, but he may also have friends from Poland who can be introduced to the reader while he is still in Warsaw. These Polish characters might include a love interest, Anna, and a best friend, Pavel. Within the squadron, Jan could have an English commanding officer, Wilson, as well as an American fellow pilot called Walsh. There might also be a radio operator, Rachel, who could perhaps be a British love interest. If we are introducing them, we should bear in mind that conflict between Jan and the other characters will be useful, at least initially. If Jan meets Pavel while they are escaping from Poland, he may be frustrated by Pavel's pacifism, which prevents him from helping to deal with a German patrol. If Jan knows Anna in Warsaw, perhaps she has a very low opinion of him because of his immaturity when they were students together. When Jan arrives at his squadron, maybe he inadvertently offends Wilson and Rachel.

While you do want to give a clear sense of the characters early in the novel, be aware that you don't have to tell everything about them the very first time we meet them. Too much information all at once can be difficult for the reader to absorb. It can also be a little boring. Some characters, however, will be fairly straightforward and their personality can be established almost immediately. For example, Jan might have a fitter – Thomas – who looks after his aircraft; a relatively uncomplicated character who is cheerful, hardworking and devoted to Jan. Thomas may be an important character in the novel but he might not need to be more than he first appears. Other characters will be more complex. For example, Walsh, the American pilot, could appear to be brave and fearless initially but, perhaps due to the trauma of his experiences, he may turn out to be anything but. Pavel may seem to be a rather hapless young man when he first appears but he might be a very talented poet who has lost his voice or perhaps he has a secret in his past that when revealed, will alter Jan's, and the reader's, perception of him. One way to give your novel interest and momentum in these early pages is to hint that the other characters are not all they seem and that there are hidden aspects to their personalities and secrets in their past. Anna, for example, could have been a member of the Communist Party who is confused by the Soviet invasion of the Eastern part of Poland, but we probably would want to show her confusion, without revealing its cause until later. If the reader is aware there is something withheld about a character, they will be intrigued and will, hopefully, want to read on to find out what it is.

Have you established and defined the dramatic worlds that confine the novel?

We discussed dramatic worlds earlier in the chapter so we probably don't need to go back over the concept again in too much detail. With a more static novel, where the characters and setting remain constant, it is often the case that there is a single dramatic world. If a novel is set in a 1930s country house, the characters and what connects them can be fixed from the first chapter with no change in the cast or the location until the last page. In Jan's novel, though, there will probably be several dramatic worlds as he and his story move forward, both in time and geographically, and his situation changes. The main ones will be the fighter squadron Jan is part of and the wider community of Polish exiles to which he also belongs. Jan may find he is at odds with his squadron, at least initially, because he feels that it is amateurish and, as a foreigner, he is not welcomed. He may want to be more aggressive in his flying than Wilson, the squadron leader, can permit, knowing he has to conserve his planes and pilots for future battles, or it could be the other way round with Wilson seeming callous about the high number of casualties. Walsh, meanwhile, may see the whole thing as an adventure and not take things seriously. The likelihood is these viewpoints will converge as the story progresses but – at least initially – their different views of what the squadron is for will cause conflict. In the Polish community, Jan is probably keen to fight for the liberation of his homeland, whereas Anna's Communist leanings push her in a different direction, while Pavel's pacifism may frustrate the others, at least to begin with. There could also be other dramatic worlds that Jan finds himself in as the story changes. Earlier we discussed a potential opening scene where Jan is shot down and captured in a wood. If we let this part of the story play out, he could find himself in a prisoner of war camp instead of being executed as he feared. This will create a new dramatic world, with new characters, all of whom have different interests and agendas, depending on whether they are a guard, a potential escapee, an informant or someone who just wants to see out the war in relative safety. By placing these characters in conflict with Jan's aim, in one way or another, our story will have lots of options as to how to proceed.

Have you established the aims and motivations of each of your characters?

Some of your characters' motivations and agendas will stem from their differing interests in the dramatic world you place them in, but by no means all. Jan's drive to be with Rachel and Anna for example, will be due to his being attracted to them, not because of the dramatic worlds through which they are connected to him. As mentioned before, when you are developing the central character and deciding on their motivation and aims over the course of your novel, it's worth considering how these might create conflict with others around them.

Many of your characters' motivations will be straightforward, at least in the first part of your novel but, as with their personalities, it is worth looking at ways to make them more complex and also to look for ways in which they may change as the story progresses. Anna, Jan's Polish love interest, may want to be with him, which can be revealed in the first part of the novel, but it might later emerge that she is already in a relationship with another man to whom she feels she should remain loyal. Similar conflicting motivations could exist for other important characters. Rachel, Jan's British love interest, might keep her distance from a fighter pilot because her friend's fiancée was shot down, but at the same time be drawn to Jan. She may also be aware of Jan's relationship with Anna. Wilson, the squadron leader, might feel duty bound as an officer to command his men to attack enemy aircraft when massively outnumbered, but at the same time be doing his best to ensure they are properly prepared and equipped to fight and doing everything within his power to protect them. To his men, he may seem cold and demanding at first, but later in the novel it could become clear he has resisted the more suicidal orders strongly and continues to do so.

Have you made the central character's objective clear?

It is important to make clear as soon as possible what your central character wants to achieve over the course of the novel. If it isn't apparent that the central character, and therefore the story, has a clear direction, then your novel may also lack direction and, therefore, momentum. The objective doesn't have to be fixed, though, and can change quite early on. For example, if we were to start Jan's novel before the war breaks out, he might be concentrating on passing some crucial exams for his degree and be oblivious to the approaching signs of conflict. That focus on the exams can introduce some early tension and momentum which will help you establish his character in a more engaging way, even if the exams are not central to the story. Once the war starts, of course, Jan's objective will be to flee to Britain and that goal will keep the story moving forward. Once he arrives, however, he may have a new objective, which is to join the RAF. His general objective remains to fight the Germans, but introducing partial objectives and obstacles that need to be overcome will help the story move forward from an early stage.

Bear in mind too that your central character can have more than one objective (and probably should). For example, Jan may also want to enter into a relationship with Anna, or find a missing brother or write poetry, and his attempts to achieve all of these aims can easily run side by side with the main storyline. They don't all have to appear in the first act (the main one should, however). Once any objective is identified, it is possible to place circumstances and characters in the way of your central character achieving it; thereby providing the obstacles and challenges that make the second act work well dramatically.

Is there a moment where the central character fully engages with the story?

Your central character is generally the most important factor in making the novel appeal to the reader. Your reader experiences the story, most probably, through the central character's experiences and emotions. The reader will be pleased when the central character is doing well and concerned when they are in peril. The central character's actions, and reactions, are also a major factor in creating momentum for your story. What the central character decides to do when faced with new information and events will shape how the story progresses. For example, if they approach the door to a house and enter, the story goes one way. If they choose to remain outside, it goes in another.

In order to make the difficult decisions that will push the story forward, the central character has to care about what they are trying to achieve. We need to use the early part of the story to give them sufficient incentive to overcome the challenges and obstacles that make up the second act. In Jan's story, therefore, we want him to be enthusiastic about his objective of fighting the Nazis. In order for this to happen, the story has to give him reasons to want to fight them. Starting the novel with an air raid on Warsaw and following it with other examples of Nazi actions that directly affect him and those he loves will go some distance to achieving this aim. The more your central character is engaged, the more likely they are to take risks and to persevere in adversity in the rest of the novel. In addition, the more your central character cares about their objective, the more your reader will, too.

Building up of incentives leads to a moment where the central character fully engages with the story. Sometimes, this occurs when they acquire information that makes them see their situation in a different light. For example, in a novel where a lawyer is representing a client who has been accused of murder, the inciting incident might be when the lawyer uncovers evidence that strongly suggests that their client is innocent. The novel might have prepared the lawyer for this information before this point by giving them indications of their client's good character and perhaps creating an emotional connection between them.

In Jan's novel, we will have been building up to his decision to go to Britain to fight the Germans, but the moment where he engages fully might be when his mother, reluctant up to this point, gives her blessing and support to his leaving. Or, alternatively, it might be when he arrives home to find that the Germans have arrested his parents and are looking for him, so that he has no choice but to leave. Or, perhaps more dramatically, he may find that his home with his parents inside, has been destroyed in a German air raid.

This moment of commitment generally comes toward the end of the first act and marks the moment where the story moves forward to the second act, or the middle of your novel.

How long does it take?

First acts can be relatively short and your story may be the better for it. If you are efficient about introducing the characters, the setting and the objective, then there is no reason why you shouldn't move on quickly to the obstacles and challenges of the second act. If, however, you find that you still have not reached the middle part of your story after eighty pages (which is approaching a quarter of a 350-page novel), then you should be concerned. Your reader will have a certain amount of patience for the introduction part of your story, but it will be finite. The second act is where the story picks up pace so it's probably best to get your reader there sooner rather than later.

Act two: the middle

If we look back at the diagram on page 115 representing the heightening of drama in the novel, it shows a gradual escalation through the first act which becomes steeper in the second act, until it reaches a peak towards the end of the novel. Whereas the first act, as mentioned above, probably shouldn't be more than about a quarter of your story (and is often much less), your second act should generally take up at least half (175 pages of a 350 page novel) of your narrative, and sometimes a little more. The first act is relatively easy – most writers will have a good idea of the characters and setting when they start their story. The second act can be more difficult, however, as this is where the writer has to make their characters start working together to tell the story they have in mind. Where the writer has not thought the story through sufficiently, they often find themselves running out of steam somewhere around page 64 (not entirely a joke: page 64 is a bit like a Bermuda Triangle where promising stories go missing without trace). Page 64 (or one nearby) is where writers discover that they do not have sufficient story to fill the 300-odd pages that remain before the novel's end. However, with a little bit of creative thinking, this is a problem that can be fixed.

Does your central character have a clear objective their story is aiming towards?

One of my favourite films is *I Know Where I'm Going*, and it's a title I have written on a piece of paper above my desk. It's there to remind me that if I don't know where the story is going, then neither will the characters and nor will the reader. I may have more than one central character or I may have a group of characters that the novel follows but the point is the same: I need to know what the characters are trying to achieve. The central character may have more than one objective over the course of the story, so Jan might want to woo Anna, as well as achieve victory over the Nazis and liberate his country and, perhaps, study part-time for a medical degree. Not all of these objectives will carry the same weight, and not all will be achieved, but the second act of Jan's novel is going to be all about him trying to achieve them. Once we know what Jan wants to achieve, we can construct the conflicts, challenges, obstacles and circumstances that will make his achieving his objectives more difficult. If your novel is running out of steam at page 64, it's probably because the objective has not been clearly defined.

How do you use conflict between the characters?

Once it has been established where the central character is going, we need to look at the other characters and consider how they can be placed between them and their destination. We should have prepared for this by establishing the aims and motivations of each of the important characters in the first act and ensuring that they are in opposition to the central character's aims but now we need to think about *specific* ways in which these characters will make the central character's path more challenging. I've explained elsewhere about the various ways in which the other characters (see Chapter 5) can make the central character's journey towards the climax more difficult. In summary, they don't necessarily have to be in direct opposition to the central character achieving their goal, although there will often be at least one character who fulfils that role. The conflict provided by other characters can be more indirect, in that rather than deliberately trying to block outright the central character's progress they can get in the way in some other manner, force the central character to change the direction of their progress, distract the central character from their goal or make any number of other interventions that have a similar effect.

In terms of Jan's novel, having the central character's objective clear in your mind is crucial in terms of plotting. If Jan's objective is to fight and defeat the Germans, then the first stage on Jan's path will be to get to Britain. Once we know that, we can arrange the characters he will interact with on his journey either to directly oppose his efforts, or make the journey more difficult in some way or perhaps to assist his journey but alter it. Jan's uncle, for example, may give him the money for the journey to Britain, and since travelling by train is impossible, introduce him to a man who can drive him to the Czech border. The driver may betray Jan to the Germans, so that Jan only barely escapes. It can be at this point he meets Pavel, our pacifist poet, who is also trying to cross the border. Jan may find his compatriot Pavel influencing him to take different approaches to problems they face during their journey. Rather than killing a sentry who bars their way, Pavel may find a non-violent approach to the obstacle. If Pavel is nearly captured, Jan may have to go back to rescue him. These characters are prompting Jan to take actions he would not attempt otherwise, forcing him to make difficult decisions and take risks which will hopefully hold the reader's attention much more effectively than if everyone he met helped him to reach his destination with minimal effort.

Does your central character have any internal issues that need to be overcome?

Not all of the problems facing your central character will be external. As noted earlier, giving your central character a weakness, a personality flaw or some other internal restriction can operate as yet another barrier to their progress that will need to be overcome. The issue could be practical, such as Jan not speaking English or having a problem with his eyes that needs to be fixed before he can become a pilot, or it could be more intimate, such as a lack of confidence, immaturity or a quick temper. It could well be that the central character has issues from their past that need to be addressed. For example, if a central character was abused as a child, then they may need to come to terms with that trauma before they can commit to being a parent. Or perhaps the central character has problems arising from addiction, mental illness, physical illness, physical disability, physical appearance and any other number of other factors. All of these, in various ways, can impede their moving forward. If your central character has an issue that needs to be tackled, then it should be fairly straightforward to work the overcoming of that problem into your story. For example, if Jan drinks too much due to the stress of flying and it begins to affect his performance, then perhaps Rachel, having seen how alcohol has affected other young pilots, will help him overcome it. If Jan is badly injured by crash landing in the forest, then overcoming his injuries and returning to the air could be an interesting part of his story.

Other sources of obstacles and challenges

Useful difficulties for the central character can arise in other ways as well. The more challenging you make the setting in which your story takes place, the more likely it will create substantial problems which the central character will need to deal with in due course. Let us use a prisoner of war camp as an example. If the camp was in or on the outskirts of a city, once the character gets over the boundary there can be places to hide, food to be had and people to help him. If the camp is located in the middle of a desert, the escapee will have none of those advantages and an environment which is potentially fatal. In contrast to this, while a journey to the post office would indeed be more difficult and exciting if it takes place in the midst of a hurricane, you have to use common sense as to whether this is a good idea in the context of your story as a whole. *Pride and Prejudice*, for example, works perfectly well without a zombie apocalypse – even if *Pride and Prejudice and Zombies* was a very entertaining tribute.

In Jan's novel, the fact that it is set in a world war will create endless opportunities to make Jan's path to the end of the novel more perilous. There will also be opportunities to use the surroundings to make individual challenges more difficult. If he has to escape Poland in mid-winter, his journey to London will be less straightforward. Individual tasks along the way can also be made more difficult if:

- he has to fly his aeroplane in fog, during a storm or at night;
- he needs to meet Anna in London while on leave, but is caught in an air raid;
- in the climate of suspicion and apprehension, he is mistaken for a German spy because of his accent.

Are there a series of obstacles and challenges – and do they increase in difficulty?

Once you have plotted out the potential difficulties that your central character needs to face, they should probably to be arranged or adjusted to ensure that there is an escalation in intensity of drama throughout the second act rather than something more erratic. Essentially, you don't want to reach peaks of drama too early in the second act (or even the first act) which will be difficult to surpass. If, for example, you were to have a very dramatic confrontation in the beginning of the second act in which several of the important characters die and your central character is seriously injured, then there would probably have to be a recovery period where some of the momentum would go out of the story. That's not to say that you can't have very dramatic events early in the second act but you need to be careful they don't undermine the flow of the narrative. It may be, of course, that the obstacles and events of your second act follow a chronological order that is difficult to adjust. If this is the case, consider taking some of the intensity out of the earlier events and increasing the intensity of those later in the story.

In Jan's story, the second act could start with his escape to Britain. We would probably focus on the dramatic events, such as being betrayed by the driver and having to make his way across mountains in mid-winter or breaking through a border checkpoint. Less important events, such as a train journey through a neutral country, can be skipped over – unless, of course, the train is boarded by soldiers looking to intern escaping Poles. On arriving in London, the drama might initially be a little quieter while he goes through training and meets up with Anna again. We could, however, create difficulties between him and the other trainees due to his frustration and this conflict could push him to the point of failure, with his commanding officer recommending he not be passed. Jan might surmount this obstacle through a humble apology and an act of bravery during an air raid. Once he becomes a fighter pilot, the opportunities for challenges to his path will increase and they might include being initially unwelcome within his squadron, crashing an airplane due to his own recklessness (and being held responsible) and having to overcome an injury that might affect his ability to fly. In addition, there can be various air battles and near-misses to keep the story moving along. Once Jan has mastered flying and become a valued member of the squadron, perhaps rising to command it, then the final obstacle could involve his escaping from a prisoner of war camp and making his way back to England.

The developments in the second act of the novel will not be limited to Jan's fighting however. Jan has at least three significant relationships: with Anna; with Rachel; and with his pacifist friend Pavel, who may serve as Jan's conscience. The dynamics of these relationships will likely change over the course of the novel with barriers to the romantic relationships preventing their early success, and with Jan and Pavel's relationship coming under strain before eventually reaching an amicable equilibrium. Each of these relationships can be largely separate to the main story, Jan's fighting the Nazis, but they can intersect with it at various times. For example, because Rachel is stationed at Jan's airfield, she can help with his English, point out to him how his own behaviour has harmed his relationships with the squadron and perhaps provide support when he is injured.

Is there a midpoint event?

Although an escalating series of obstacles, challenges and dramatic events leading towards the novel's climax can work well as a general structure for the second act of a novel, it is also worth considering whether your novel should have a midpoint event that changes its direction. This can be presented as a false ending, where it appears that the central character has been defeated or has succeeded (although neither will be the case). It can also work as a revelation that alters the central character's understanding of the story so far and what they need to achieve. Often the midpoint event will raise the difficulties of making their way to the final objective while increasing the central character's desire to do so. The benefit of a false ending is that it creates the momentum and drama that you would expect when approaching the end of a story which can tighten up what might otherwise be a slack period in the middle of the novel. In crime fiction, if a detective believes that they have discovered the killer in a murder case, it might turn out that they were mistaken and realising their mistake will reveal a far greater conspiracy than they were previously aware of. In Jan's story, it could be his promotion to Squadron Leader and imminent marriage to Anna but when they are caught in an air raid, as mentioned above, Anna may be tragically killed and Jan left (temporarily) blind. Midpoint events work best when there is an emotional impact, which there clearly would be in Jan's case. The death and blindness will likely be traumatic, not least because the injury will affect his ability to fight the Germans, and the grief and anger may change his personality. Anna's death will, however, inspire him to overcome the physical challenges of his injury in order to get back to fighting the Nazis. The midpoint event may also encourage central characters to examine themselves and adjust their behaviour. If, up until this point, Jan has been impetuous and immature, he may now be more focussed and conscious of his responsibilities not only to himself but also to those around him. He could find support from Rachel and Pavel, and that support may overcome previous disagreements and misunderstandings and begin the transformation of those relationships into their final state.

Not every novel needs a midpoint event but they can be very useful for injecting impetus. In addition, changing the direction of the story, which such events often do, will probably cause the reader to engage with the story in a new way. By making Jan suffer through a traumatic event, we can evoke sympathy for his injuries and his grief, while also creating interest in how he is going to overcome them in order to reach the real end of the story.

Is the pace too frenetic?

If your second act is a relentless series of dramatic events, readers may feel at exhausted and/or confused. Remember, then, to have quieter scenes after very dramatic incidents so that the reader and the important characters can take stock and reflect. These scenes will also allow the central character, and the other important characters, to reveal their emotional reactions to the recent dramatic event and consider the possible implications. If Jan is left blind after the air raid, it will be natural to have some scenes immediately afterwards where he is recovering. These can show the emotional impact of the event, perhaps leading to him engaging in destructive behaviour such as drinking, before he gathers himself and considers how to go forward. When he is shot down and captured, there may be a quieter passage afterwards where he considers how close he was to death and observes his new situation with a view to escaping. Good central characters are emotional entities and are affected by the events they experience. If they don't show any reactions to key events, whether traumatic, more joyful or something else entirely, then it's probably going to undermine their credibility.

Quieter scenes are also useful when there is a change of location or setting which needs to be explained to the reader, or new characters are introduced. More dramatic scenes can achieve these aims also, but sometimes it's good to take a breath and explore other aspects of the story.

Is your central character at genuine risk?

When constructing the events that will make up the middle of your novel, it's worth bearing in mind that one way of calibrating the escalating drama is to consider the degree of risk that the central character is in. The risk can be physical, and clearly in Jan's novel there will be a fair amount of this, but it can also be emotional, or reputational, or perhaps a danger to the central character's economic position. If we think back to the family drama example we explored earlier, with the troubled relationship between a mother and her daughter, the central character's emotional wellbeing may what is at risk as relationships go awry. The daughter may also lose her job, which would affect her financial situation, and her unhappiness may lead to bad decisions in her love life, leading to an unwanted pregnancy. She might go through the whole novel without being in physical danger of any kind but that doesn't mean that the dangers she faces won't matter to her and to the reader.

Does your central character drive the story?

This is another factor to bear in mind when plotting the key events of your novel, and particularly the second act. Whether you have one central character, more than one or a group of characters that your novel follows, it is important that their decisions and action should drive the story wherever possible. It is the central character's story, even if there is more than one of them, therefore they need to decide its direction, rather than have the story happening to them because of other people's actions and decisions. Obviously, this isn't always the case. There will be other characters with their own agendas who will take actions explicitly designed to inhibit the central character's progress, but it's sensible that most of the positive developments in the story, in other words where it moves forward, will be caused by the central character in some way. If, for example, in the course of Jan and Pavel's escape from Poland, all of the important actions and decisions were to be made by Pavel, then the principle that it is Jan's story would be under threat. Similarly, if there are problems to be solved, information to be obtained or any challenges that need to be overcome, it should probably be the central character who provides the solution, asks the question or takes the important step forward.

Is there a significant event that leads to the final ordeal?

All of the surmounted obstacles, key revelations, temporary reverses and other occurrences of the second act are leading toward the final challenge that takes place at the end of the novel. To make that final challenge as significant as possible, we need to ensure that the central character's failure to overcome it will lead to the greatest tension. Often that means changing the direction of the story so that whereas the central character had been approaching their objective, they will now find themselves facing one last (perhaps unexpected) challenge or maybe realising that their presumed objective is now no longer the one that they need to achieve, and that they should focus on something else instead. In a romantic novel, say, the central character may realise that they don't love the character they have been pursing up until that point but have actually fallen for another character altogether. There will probably be a trigger event for this, perhaps the false love revealing their true nature, or a loss of contact with the true love, revealing the central character's real feelings. Once faced with the reality of those feelings, the central character will be at risk of not achieving personal happiness and, in the final act, will have to take whatever action is necessary to resolve the situation. In Jan's novel, following Anna's death, he could be approaching success with Rachel and also anticipating the defeat of the Nazis. If we create a misunderstanding, perhaps over a perceived relationship with another man, that causes a break between Jan and Rachel and then have him shot down and captured by the SS who want to execute him, we place him at severe risk of failure. If he discovers in his pocket, after he has been shot down, a letter from Rachel which explains that the other man is a doctor cousin and reveals that she is pregnant, then he has a strong reason for facing the final, all-or-nothing, confrontation.

Act three: the end

The third, and final, act of your novel is where your story comes to a close. This should involve a final confrontation of some description where the central character is not certain of achieving their objective as well as substantial risk to their wellbeing, whether it is physical, emotional or otherwise. It is also the part of the novel where you answer any outstanding questions the reader may have, as well as tidying up any loose ends. Finally, it is often the part of the novel where we tell the reader what happens to the characters after the story ends.

Is there a final challenge?

The final challenge is the point at which the central character (or the characters whose story the novel follows) either reach their end goal, or fail. Your central character may not, of course, be destined to succeed and many novels will be about a character's ultimate failure, whether it be glorious or tragic. Many novels end with success for the central character, but it sometimes comes at a cost which may make the achievement of it somewhat bittersweet. The final challenge is unlikely to be a single scene, although it can be. More often, it will be a series of events which share the common aim of overcoming the significant obstacle that the final challenge represents. If you were writing a crime novel or thriller, for example, it could be made up of a chase, the liberation of a kidnapped loved one, a fight, and the final capture of a killer. In this example, the central character may be on the point of failure when a piece of luck or a last-minute intervention saves them. In a romantic novel, the object of the central character's affections may be about to marry someone else, leave the country, join a religious order or take some other irrevocable step which means the romance is doomed. The central character may then have to undertake a dangerous journey, renounce their inheritance, or swim across shark-infested waters in order to persuade the loved one to stay and be happy with them. Not all endings are quite so dramatic but if the central character believes all is lost if they fail, and if there are practical obstacles which have to be overcome, then the final confrontation will be dramatic. If we were looking at Jan's novel, where he has been shot down and captured, we could have him risk a dangerous escape, make his way back to Britain while being chased by the Nazis and reunite with Rachel with a whole series of dangers and problems along the way. The backdrop of Jan's story gives ample opportunity to make these quite extreme and he could be about to be killed by a German patrol when some partisans intervene to rescue him. He is, after all, allowed a little bit of luck at the end.

What is important in the final challenge is that the central character really cares about the outcome. If they don't, the reader may not either. In other words, aside from the risks that they face and the danger of failing to achieve their objective, it works well if there is an emotional benefit of success, and an emotional loss if there is failure.

Does your novel have, or need, a final twist or surprise?

Another thing to consider for the end of your novel is a potential further twist after what appears to be the final challenge is achieved. This is more common in novels that involve uncovering information, such as a crime novel, a spy story or a thriller. It seems as though the criminal has been captured or the traitor uncovered but there is one final missing piece to the puzzle, which leads to either a further challenge or one last revelation. If it seems that the killer has been captured but in interrogation they deny one of the murders, then perhaps that will reveal a second killer. If the traitor has been uncovered and shot dead, the central character might suspect that the traitor couldn't have worked alone and this realisation lead to the revelation that his partner is also a traitor. This kind of twist doesn't happen in every novel – I'm not sure a twist would be necessary or useful in Jan's novel – but it is something to bear in mind. The questions in this part of the chapter are a menu rather than a formula, so consider which may help you end your novel in a satisfying way for the reader.

Does the ending offer a pleasing conclusion to the character's emotional journey?

Pleasing, in this context, doesn't mean happy – instead it means satisfying from a reader's perspective. The events of your story will probably have changed the central character and they will have learned something about themselves and about their place in the world. The likelihood is that your central character will be a better person, although this might not always be the case. For example, where a central character has followed a downward moral trajectory over the course of the story, the ending may involve them reaching their lowest point. What is important is that you ensure that there is an emotional journey for the central character and that it ends in a logical and credible way, with the central character displaying change in their personality and emotional state. If Jan starts the novel angry at the Germans, he may end the novel in a more conciliatory frame of mind, now that the war has finished, tired of violence and killing and happy to be together with Rachel and their child. He will have been matured by the story's events, gained self-confidence and an appreciation of the things that are important to him personally. It's often the case that the central character has to change in order to achieve their objective. In *Pride and Prejudice*, both Elizabeth and Darcy have to overcome their own personality flaws in order to be together. In Jan's novel, it could be that his growing maturity and efforts to work with his comrades and superiors, rather than on his own, will be what persuades Rachel to commit to him and enables him to escape from the Germans.

How do your sub-plots end? Do they feed into the main plot in a satisfying way?

As with the central character's emotional journey, it is worth identifying the sub-plots in your novel, ensuring that they have a logical progression and that they end. If, for example, Rachel did not appear again after the misunderstanding at the end of the second act which led to her rejecting Jan, then the reader would be perplexed about why the novel spent so much time on a relationship that ultimately fizzled out. That doesn't mean that the relationship between Jan and Rachel has to end positively but it does need to reach a credible conclusion. If, after returning from being captured, Jan and Rachel meet and agree to go their separate ways, we will at least have an ending. Sub-plots, like the main plot, generally follow a three-act structure, and if they don't, you probably need to consider why that is the case and whether their being more structured would help the novel as a whole. Sub-plots generally also run alongside, and within, the main plot. In Rachel's case, her presence at the airfield where Jan is based means that she could play a helpful role in the main plot itself, as would Pavel in Jan's escape from Poland at the beginning of the novel. Other sub-plots are more related to characterisation and the central character's emotional journey: this would probably be true of Jan's relationship with Anna, whose main function will be to show Jan's character and how it changes, although Anna's death will also provide Jan with motivation to persevere through the challenges of the later parts of the novel.

If you don't have a three-act structure – what do you have?

Your story doesn't *have to have* a beginning, middle and end – but it is advisable. This chapter, as with the rest of this guide, is more of a series of options than a set of firm rules. However, if your novel is going to follow an alternative structure, consider how it will be received by the reader. If there is a possibility they will be confused, consider how you can reduce the chances of that happening. If there is a lack of conflict or a pattern of dramatic events, think about ways to compensate for that.

Summary

To consolidate what has been discussed in this chapter, use the question prompts below to create a three-act plot for a crime novel. These questions are a guide, not a strict template.

ACT ONE

1. Briefly describe the crime.
2. Who are the principal suspects in the investigation?
3. How is the protagonist introduced?
4. What are the major external obstacles facing the central character (e.g. grumpy/obstructive boss)?
5. What are the major internal obstacles facing the central character (e.g. depressed, alcoholic, unrequited love)?
6. Establish the agendas (preferably competing) of several of your principal characters. (Aim for three or four characters including the protagonist.)
7. Create an INCITING INCIDENT with which to end the act. A twist/revelation/game-changing moment which prompts the protagonist to embark on a challenging path.

ACT TWO

This is the hardest act to plot, but is chiefly about uncovering layers of evidence, developing intrigue and confronting mounting obstacles. The act ideally crescendos with the protagonist on the brink of a huge ordeal which will test him/her to the outer limits.

1. What are the sources of rising tension for the central character? What are the forces ranged against him/her?
2. A further reversal – an event which pushes the protagonist further out on a limb (e.g. a second murder, an unexpected piece of evidence, conflict with another character).
3. Developments/conflicts with other principal characters (changes in competing agendas, for example).
4. Does the central character find unexpected support/assistance from another character?
5. A revelation/situation that alters the course of story and applies even greater pressure on the protagonist. This could be an intensification of the story through the revealing of the truth layer.
6. A situation which pushes the protagonist to their outer limits. (Perhaps this forces them to confront the possibility of inhabiting the inverse of the positive value they represent.)

ACT THREE

Act three of a crime novel involves the final confrontation, a final twist and an emotional resolution that ties the story strands together. Some stories manage to pull off the trick of the protagonist completing a journey of personal redemption as well as successfully concluding the investigation.

1. What is the final confrontation of the action sequence? Make sure it takes the protagonist far out on a limb – the danger need not be physical, (e.g. the protagonist could face humiliation and dismissal rather than violence).
2. What is at stake in the final confrontation for the protagonist and for other important central characters?
3. What is the revelation/dramatic conclusion to the final confrontation?
4. Where will my protagonist go from here?

CHAPTER 7

Writing scenes

Your novel, if it is to be a successful undertaking, will be made up of a series of scenes designed to tell your story in the best way possible. Your job then, as a writer, is to choose scenes that keep your novel moving forward and give the reader all the information they require to understand the story from start to finish. Because of the way most novels are structured – with a beginning, a middle and an end as we discovered in the previous chapter – you will also find that these scenes have a logical order and that particular events (and the scenes in which they appear) will belong in predictable parts of the novel. For example, you will probably introduce the important characters and the setting at the beginning of the novel and you probably won't want to give away the ending in the first chapter.

Your novel is not just about events and information, however, although these do form the backbone of most stories. You also will need to look at each scene you choose with a critical eye and consider ways in which it can be improved to help the story, such as characterisation, setting and atmosphere. Each scene will have its own needs from a storytelling perspective, and will have to be constructed accordingly. Some will be dramatic, some thrilling and some much quieter, focussed on improving the reader's knowledge of the characters' motivations and desires.

Chapters and scenes

You'll have noticed that we're discussing scenes rather than chapters and it's worth explaining why. A scene, for our purposes, is an episode in a novel where something happens, generally in the same place, often defined by a continuous time period and usually with the same characters involved. The scene often ends when there is a shift in time, or a shift in location, or a shift in the characters that are the focus of the scene or, in short, whenever you decide to move onto the next one.

A chapter, on the other hand, is whatever passage of writing the author (or editor) says it is. Sometimes chapters are limited to a single scene or, very occasionally, a single sentence, although often they will extend over several scenes. The length can vary as well, from a few lines to seventy or eighty pages. By way of example, my first novel had twenty-eight chapters, the majority of which were made up of several scenes, and which were generally around fifteen pages long. My fourth novel, on the other hand had ninety-nine chapters, the majority of which were made up of single scenes and which varied in length from two pages to ten – in other words, they were as long as the scene they contained. Both novels are around the same number of words and contain more or less the same number of scenes, which are handled in broadly similar ways. The difference between the two is solely how I organised those scenes into chapters, and by the time I came to write the fourth novel, I had decided that there were advantages to single-scene chapters.

One reason I considered single-scene chapters to be preferable in the fourth novel, was that it was told from four different storytelling perspectives, whereas my novels up to that point has been predominately told from a single point of view. Because I was using different points of view in the fourth novel, it tended to be the case that the storytelling perspective switched at the end of a scene, and I decided it made sense to start a new chapter when I did so. There might also be some differences in *how* the reader reads a novel based on its chapter lengths and I tend to believe that shorter chapters help with pace and engagement. The shorter chapters can also help with clarity, as in this case where there were multiple storytelling perspectives. Again, this is my opinion – but it isn't something that can be scientifically established as writing is not a science. You'll have to come to your own conclusions as to whether

I am right or wrong and, in any event, choose the approach that you think works best for your novel.

The most important factor in deciding how to arrange the scenes in your novel is not chapter length but whether the scenes it contains earn their place and allow the story to be told in the way you want it to be told. If they pass this test, then all you have to do is write it and structure it to do its job in the best way possible. Simple.

Purpose

Writing a novel is often about asking questions and considering possibilities. The important question that you probably need to answer before you write the first word of any scene is what its purpose is in the overall story. Scenes can fulfil many different functions in a novel but knowing the narrative essence of the scene – the reason why it *has* to be in the novel – will probably tell you a lot about how the scene has to be written, what has to be in it and what you can leave out. Perhaps the easiest way to think of a scene's purpose is to identify the reason why it can't be discarded; if its absence will have no effect on the novel, then discarding it is probably the right decision.

What narrative purposes, then, justify a scene's inclusion in your novel? There is no exact formula and different novels will have different narrative requirements. However, here are some that probably do deserve inclusion:

- scenes that introduce the setting in which the novel will take place or which establish atmosphere;
- scenes that introduce key characters or, once they have been introduced, tell us something about them that is important to the story;
- scenes where a key event occurs or a key piece of information is revealed that moves the story forward or sends it in a new direction;

- scenes where a challenge, obstacle or danger to the central character is introduced;
- scenes which create anticipation and expectation;
- climax scenes where the character must overcome one last obstacle, the biggest yet, in order to reach their objective;
- scenes that come after the climax which serve to tie up loose ends and confirm that the objective has been achieved.

This is not an exhaustive list and there will be, in practice, quite a lot of overlap as a scene may fulfil different story purposes at the same time; very occasionally, it will fulfil none of them at all. What it must do, though, is help the story in some way.

Whether a scene's purpose justifies its inclusion will also depend, in some cases, on where the scene is placed in the novel. Scenes which focus solely on atmosphere, setting or world-building are usually dealt with early in the novel. For example, if you place a scene which gives important practical information about the setting of the story towards the end of your novel, it will probably no longer be necessary, will slow the novel down at a point where you are generally looking to speed it up and possibly be confusing for the reader. Information about setting or place is therefore much better included towards the beginning, even if its importance becomes apparent only later on. For similar reasons, it's best to introduce important characters early on. Even if they can't actually appear until the closing chapters, information about them should probably be seeded well before that so that their arrival does not seem contrived.

Let's consider some examples of scenes which would justify inclusion and ones which would probably not. In order to do this, imagine we are writing a novel that revolves around a romance between two characters called Harry and Sally, taking place on a tropical island:

- **Setting and dramatic world.** We will probably have several scenes towards the beginning of the novel where we establish the geography of the island, as well as any important story information – such as, for example, that it is subject to very violent hurricanes – which may become relevant later in the novel. We might want to spend some time at this point establishing the atmosphere of the island which is perhaps very laid back and friendly. We will also likely spend a little time describing the homes in which Harry and Sally live, how the island works as a community, particularly if there are rules of behaviour or issues that the reader will need to know about (for example, a new marina is planned for visiting yachts which would damage a coral reef Harry plans to study). Scenes whose purpose relates to the setting and the dramatic world in which the story will take place are good to get out of the way early on in the story as they are generally a little slow and, as you might expect, more focussed on giving the reader information related to their purpose than drama.

- **Introducing the characters.** We will probably want to combine the scenes in which we introduce the island and its community with scenes where we introduce Harry and Sally and the other important characters. If Harry is new to the island, we'll probably use his point of view as he'll be able to notice things about the setting, and the people he meets, that would seem contrived from characters that already know them. As well as meeting the important characters, we will also want to give the reader useful information about their previous lives. If Sally is from the most influential family on the island, and the driving force behind the marina development, the reader will need to know about this early on. If Harry is a keen sailor, that might also be useful to know, as it may give him some expertise in the location of the new marina, which could come in useful for the story at a later stage.
- **But be careful that the information you give is relevant.** We will probably not need a scene describing Harry's schooldays in Aberdeen unless they relate directly to the story. Likewise, there is

no point spending a lot of time describing a beautiful beach if it is not important to the story. On the other hand, it will probably be useful to describe a beach beside the coral reef which will also be affected by the marina, particularly if potential damage to it will be significant to the story.

- **Establishing the central character's objective.** We will obviously want to include the scene where Harry and Sally meet for the first time, as this will be an event around which the whole novel will revolve. However, if we look at it from a story perspective, most fictional romances are not straightforward and if Harry and Sally fall head over heels with each other immediately, and there are no barriers to the relationship, then our novel would probably be more of a short story. So, while we need a scene which has their meeting as its purpose because it establishes the objective of the novel (Harry and Sally living happily ever after), we will probably want to combine it with a complication. Perhaps, taking *Romeo and Juliet* as an example, we will have Harry and the local environmentalists meeting Sally and the local business community. If Harry and Sally continue to clash with regard to the marina, then that is at least one barrier which they will have to overcome. We might also use the scene to introduce a rival for Sally's affections, a slightly slimy lawyer called Ricky who represents the marina interests. He will be another obstacle that Harry and Sally will need to get past.
- **Challenges and obstacles (and solutions).** Once the objective is set, we will probably want the novel to take on an increasing momentum. One way in which we will do this is by including scenes which establish challenges and obstacles that the potential lovers will have to deal with in different ways. These might include misunderstandings between Harry and Sally that push them apart: Harry might have his funding removed at Sally's behest, or perhaps Ricky, the lawyer, proposes to

Sally. If there are obstacles, we will also have to find ways in which to overcome them. For example, a friend of Sally's might realise that Sally and Harry would be very well suited and try to bring them together. We might also have a scene the purpose of which is to reveal that Ricky, Harry's rival, is not all that he seems. Perhaps Ricky is dishonest and will benefit from the marina being placed in that particular location or he is already secretly attached to another woman. A scene in which an alternative marina site is found, one more suited to yachts, might also be useful, particularly as this will likely be against Ricky's interests. And perhaps Harry's work on the coral reef will attract tourists, making its destruction no longer attractive to the business community and thereby solving his funding problems. It's a good idea to arrange challenges and obstacles to be progressively more difficult to overcome so that when the final one arrives it will seem, at least initially, insurmountable.

- **Foreshadow future challenges.** We may also want to include scenes featuring an approaching hurricane, which we have established earlier are a constant danger to the island. These scenes will work to create a sense of anticipation for what might happen at the end of the novel.
- **Think about the final crisis.** Our climax scenes, following our careful foreshadowing, could feature the arrival of a massive hurricane that requires Harry and Sally to work together to save each other's lives and perhaps the community. The storm might reveal the lawyer's duplicity in some way, while making Harry and Sally realise that they are destined for each other and that the marina would be better off on the other side of the island, where it would be more sheltered.
- **Tidy up loose ends.** The very last scenes could feature the lawyer being imprisoned, the marina being opened in its new location, and Harry and Sally living together happily ever after.

As mentioned above, if you have identified the purpose of your scene in the overall story, it will make it much easier to write. (It will also save you writing scenes that do not have a purpose within the story, as those will often be ones which you will have to remove at a later stage.) In addition, if you start writing knowing why this particular scene *has* to be in the novel it will, unsurprisingly, help you approach it in a positive frame of mind.

So far, so good.

Where should I start my scene?

Every novel and every scene will have different requirements so there are no hard and fast rules but it's often the case that the sooner your scene gets to its main purpose, the better. If, for example, you are writing a piece of dialogue between a central character and an acquaintance in which a key piece of information will be revealed, it may be tempting to start just before the point of the revelation without bothering with the earlier parts of the conversation or much set up. But this will depend very much on the on the kind of novel you are writing and where the scene sits within the overall story. For example, in our Harry and Sally novel (let's call it *Hurricane*), with its relaxed island setting and atmosphere, we might want to start such a scene slowly – certainly if the scene is placed towards the beginning of the novel. In this case, we could pause to take in a beautiful vista or even enjoy a cold beer before the acquaintance arrives. Kicking off the scene this way may allow us to achieve the additional purpose of creating setting and atmosphere, which are important tasks in the early stages of a novel. We could even introduce an element of humour – perhaps Harry's drink could be stolen by a beer-loving monkey – which again might fit well with the tone we want the novel to have. Even when the acquaintance arrives, we could probably justify a more roundabout start to the conversation if we haven't fully introduced either character to the reader.

If, however, we were approaching a scene like this towards the end of *Hurricane* – perhaps in the midst of the life-threatening eponymous weather event – we want to get to the information part of the conversation much more quickly. At this climax stage of the novel, we are looking for drama, excitement and momentum, having already established the setting and characters. A slow start to an exchange at this point would probably be counter-productive.

It also depends, as mentioned, on the type of novel you're writing. If, for example, you are writing a thriller, you will often be looking to create momentum from the outset so even in the early chapters you want to get to the information part of the exchange as early as you can. Obviously, there will have to be some lead-in, but you may decide this is best done as efficiently as possible and in a way that helps inject pace and drama.

Creating anticipation in the mind of the reader, on the other hand, may be a reason why you want to take your time getting to the purpose part of a scene. Where the reader is aware that a key event is about to take place, possibly involving risk, extending the build-up can work very well to increase tension. You may also want to add in elements that increase the sense of the imminent event – for example, creaking floorboards, fog and the point of view character's nervousness will all work well in a scene like this.

In summary, the approach you take will be determined by the purpose of the scene, where it is placed in the novel and what you intend for the novel as a whole. If you decide your approach based on these factors, and then execute it elegantly, efficiently and entertainingly, you probably won't go too far wrong.

Who is telling the scene?

Many novels are told entirely from one point of view and if that's the case with your novel, you can skip this bit. However, if your novel is told by multiple narrators, you will need to decide which of those storytelling perspectives works best.

Generally speaking, if your central character is present, you are probably going to want to use their point of view to tell the scene because the novel is, after all, their story. Even where a novel uses multiple storytelling voices, it will generally be predominately told by the central character or characters. Bear in mind, however, that the character 'telling' a scene can generally only record for the reader their own inner thoughts and what their senses reveal to them. This means that they can't know what other characters are thinking and nor can they see themselves, unless in some kind of reflection. If you need to get around these restrictions for some reason, then shifting the storytelling perspective to another character is a practical solution. Let's say that in *Hurricane* you want Sally to be visible in a scene early in the novel so that you can give the reader a clear physical description. In this case, using a friend's point of view is going to be an option well worth considering: ideally, choose someone who can not only describe her but also perhaps tell us a little about her past as well as her current situation. Likewise, in a conversation between a central character and a minor character, you might want to be inside a minor character's head to reveal that they are lying to the central character or to show how they feel about the central character or just to reveal the minor character's general emotional state. If you rely on the central character's external observation of the minor character, this information can only be guessed at through the central character's observations, and you may have story reasons for not wanting the central character to be aware of the information in any way. For example, in *Hurricane*, if Ricky is having coffee with Sally, then using his perspective to tell the scene will allow you to reveal his nefarious plans, while allowing Sally to remain unaware of them.

If the central character is not present in a scene then you will need to decide which alternative storytelling perspective works best for the scene, and for the novel as a whole. Often this decision will be straightforward, either because there is only one perspective available, or because the character you use to tell the scene will be otherwise immediately obvious. In other scenes, the decision as to who should tell the scene may be a little bit more complex, particularly where there are several alternatives. In this situation, it's worth taking a moment to consider your options. Some questions you might want to ask yourself are:

- **Which character will have the most interesting or effective storytelling voice for the scene in question?** This will depend on what you hope to achieve with the scene. If, for example, you have a character who is observant as well as being witty, they could be useful for a scene where some social awkwardness features. In a scene featuring violence, you might take the view of a perpetrator to reveal the motivation and perhaps justification, or alternatively the view of a victim to create compassion or make the scene more emotional.
- **What does the character know?** Sometimes one of your characters will have knowledge that isn't available to the other characters in the scene, and this will shape their interpretation of the events in a useful light. If the purpose of a scene in *Hurricane* is to reveal that Ricky might be cheating during a high-stakes game of poker, then using the perspective of a friend of Harry's who is an expert card player would work well.
- **Where is the character physically placed in the scene, and will their position offer a useful view of what is going to take place?** This decision depends on how you want to tell the scene and what the purpose of the scene is. Sometimes you want to have a little distance, perhaps to show what happens in a wide angle. In other situations, you want to have your character more involved in what's taking place. For example, in *Hurricane*, if the slimy lawyer and Sally's father meet in a café where they will have a conversation in which information is revealed concerning the coral reef, then it will make sense for you to tell the scene from

the perspective of one of those two characters. However, if the purpose of the scene is to merely to make the reader aware that the two characters have met in the café but be ambiguous as to what is discussed, then you might want to use the perspective of a friend of Harry's who happens to be present but is unable to overhear. Of course, if it's important to your story that Harry knows what is discussed, but that Sally's father and the slimy lawyer are not aware that they are being listened to, then you could move Harry's friend to a closer position from where he can overhear and observe, unnoticed.

- **How important is the character to the story and is this an opportunity to find out more about them?** If an important character is present in your scene, there may be advantages to using their perspective as this can give, through their internal monologue, an insight into their personality and motivation. In other scenes, you might want to use a minor character, so that you can observe a more important character through their eyes.

One common reason to choose a non-central character's storytelling perspective is where you want to give the reader information that the central character doesn't yet have. One good example of this would be Ricky having a conversation with Sally where he purports to be affectionate and loving, but his affection is undercut by his nefarious internal plotting. This knowledge will shape the reader's understanding of the novel going forward and, because the reader (hopefully) cares about Sally's wellbeing, it will create tension and anticipation that would not have existed otherwise. If, during the conversation, Ricky suggests a trip on his yacht, the reader may be alarmed on Sally's behalf and, hopefully, keen to read on to find out what he will do. In a different novel, a central character might be unaware that a colleague is in love with them, but the reader knows, because of the colleague's narration, so you've created an ongoing tension and anticipation for the reader.

This technique, of giving the reader information that the central character doesn't have, can also be used to foreshadow dangers, revelations and other events. In each case, the reader is anticipating what will happen when the central character uncovers the reality of their situation. For example, if we were to use the slimy lawyer's perspective to tell a scene where Harry is planning a scuba dive with Sally, we might use Ricky's internal monologue to suggest that it would be a shame if the equipment were to be tinkered with. Likewise, if Sally's best friend sees Harry and Sally enjoying each other's company, the friend may notice a growing attraction that neither Harry nor Sally, nor indeed the reader, have been aware of up until this point. Even if it takes some time for this kind of knowledge to be revealed to the characters in question, the reader will be reading in anticipation of the probable implications when it does.

One last point on who is telling a scene. If a dramatic or exciting event occurs and your central character is not present, avoid telling them (and therefore the reader) about it through dialogue. Obviously, if you are writing your novel using only the central character's point of view, you may not have much choice (although it is always worth asking yourself if there is some way your character *can* be present). If, however, you are using several perspectives to tell the story, then it is probably sensible – where possible – to write the event from the perspective of someone who is part of it and who can then tell your central character about it in abbreviated form afterwards (there's no need to go into detail if the reader already knows everything). If a narrator is part of a dramatic event rather than telling it afterwards, it is nearly always going to be more engaging for the reader.

How should you start?

Scenes, like novels, often have a beginning, a middle and an end. As with the novel, we often need to set the scene up so it's generally a good idea to tell the reader as soon as possible (often in the first few sentences) who is telling the scene (that is, which character's point of view you're using), where it is taking place, which other characters are present or will soon be present and any other crucial information that the reader will expect to be told immediately (such as if someone is pointing a gun at someone else). You might also want to remind the reader of any previously discovered information that is going to be relevant to the scene. This can all be done in one or two sentences and it gets it out of the way so that you don't interrupt the action part of the scene.

Are there exceptions? As mentioned before, sometimes indicating that something or someone is present in a scene, but holding off on revealing exactly what or who, can work well to increase tension. If our central character enters an abandoned building where the reader, and the central character, suspect that a killer is hiding, then we can allow the scene to proceed for quite some time before the actual encounter. If we add in creaking floorboards, a dripping tap and a strange smell that may, or may not, be blood we will have created quite a lot of tension in the scene. It is also the case that giving some but not all of the information can be very effective in creating questions in the reader's mind. For example, if you are writing the same scene from the as yet unrevealed killer's perspective, you would probably want to obscure quite a lot of information – particularly where the scene is taking place and who the killer is and what their intentions are, but you probably would want to make it clear that they are observing the central character and use the reader's fear for their safety to increase the tension. While you might not reveal the killer's identity, you could give the reader some clues to get them thinking.

Conflict, risk, obstacles and subtext

If a scene needs enhancement, consider adding some extra ingredients: conflict, risk, obstacles and subtext can all help boost a scene's impact.

Conflict is ingredient number one. A central character is very often at odds with the majority of the other characters, to a lesser or greater extent, for most of the novel. The central character may also be at odds with the environment they find themselves in and, indeed, with themselves. This is just as well, as novels would be a bit boring if things were to go too easily for the central character. If there is no obstacle to the attraction between Harry and Sally in *Hurricane*, then it is going to be a short, and uninteresting, romance. The same applies in every genre and nearly every novel. A murder mystery without conflict, for example, means that no one will have a motive to kill the victim so there would be no murder, murderer or possible suspects. Even if we manage to overcome that problem, we'd have all the characters doing their best to help the investigator to solve the crime which would result in honesty, cooperation, support, a lack of misinformation, an absence of hidden agendas and quite a lot of very easily obtained truth. None of which are elements usually found in a murder mystery and all of which are driven by conflict between the characters.

Conflict doesn't necessarily mean your characters have to be shouting at each other on every page, however. It is sufficient to have your characters hinder each other's progress, generally by creating obstacles and challenges that make achieving their objectives more difficult, thereby forcing them into finding ways to overcome the resulting problems and resistance. If you look back at *Hurricane*, you'll find we've carefully constructed quite a lot of opposition from the characters, including Harry and Sally themselves, to their romantic relationship ever coming to pass. *Hurricane*'s story will be about resolving or at least addressing each of the conflicts, and therefore removing the obstacles that they create to the romance.

When approaching the writing of a scene, then, it's worth identifying the possible points of conflict within it. Let's take that murder mystery novel as an example and think about a scene the investigator needs to uncover a key piece of information from a witness. The simplest way to write this scene would be as a straightforward interrogation where the witness answers all the investigator's questions honestly.

However, it might be worth asking if, by introducing conflict, we can make obtaining the information more difficult. It could be helpful, for example, if we were to place the witness's life, or the life of a loved one, at risk if they disclose the information. By doing this, we have given the witness a different motivation (to *not* reveal the key information) to that of the investigator. Once we've established the differing motivations, we can then think about the strategies each of the characters will use to achieve their conflicting aims. The witness, for example, might attempt to pin the blame on an innocent person, or claim that they know nothing useful, or beg the investigator not to ask them questions that will place their loved one in danger. The investigator will then have come up with a strategy to persuade the witness to cooperate. Perhaps they will reveal the innocent person has a solid alibi, or reassure the witness as to their safety, or threaten the witness with consequences if they don't reveal the information the investigator wants. Whatever approach the investigator takes, they will obtain the same information from the scene, but by making obtaining it more difficult to do so we have hopefully made the scene more engaging dramatically.

Not all conflicts have to be substantial and events can be improved by introducing a minor element of discord. Even something as mundane as making a cup of tea can be improved by a disagreement as to how it is best done. In short, anything you can do to create differences of opinion or awkwardness for your central character, is probably going to be a useful enhancement to a scene.

Risk, or danger, is also a useful addition to a scene, particularly in the second half of a novel where most novels will require an escalation of drama and tension. The risk that you introduce doesn't necessarily need to be physical; it can also be emotional (as in risk to a character's mental wellbeing or contentment) or status-related (where the risk can be to the central character's economic or social position). Nor does the risk have to directly affect a character: for example, the risk can be to someone or something a character cares about. The risk doesn't necessarily have to be significant either. It can be just a fear of being embarrassed, making a mistake or rejection by a member of the opposite sex – although more substantial risks will often have more obvious dramatic benefits.

By way of example we might want to include a scene in *Hurricane* where Harry explains to Sally the danger that the marina will pose to the coral reef. Harry could explain the environmental consequences to Sally over a cup of coffee, or they could dive down to the reef so that he can show her its fragility firsthand. Clearly a dive in tropical waters presents all sorts of possibilities for danger, and therefore an opportunity for the characters to work together to overcome it, perhaps discovering qualities in each other that they haven't noticed up to this point at the same time. In a similar way, we could avoid physical danger but introduce something that will make the scene risky for Harry in another way. For example, we could make Harry (but not Sally) aware that his shorts have split. Harry's attempts to avoid embarrassment, while still revealing the possible damage to the reef, might work well in terms of lifting the tension in the scene. If we wanted to introduce a danger to a friend of Harry's, we could have Sally mention that her lawyer boyfriend knows someone is giving Harry information about the Marina development and is close to uncovering them. How will Harry attempt to deflect attention away from his friend?

Risk is not something you need to introduce in every scene, but it can certainly be a useful addition from time to time.

Obstacles are another ingredient that can add to a scene's effectiveness. In terms of the overall structure of the novel, the more challenging you make the central character's progress towards their final objective, the better and it is very similar when looking at individual scenes. As before, our investigator's objective in a scene may be to acquire some information and introducing an obstacle which must be dealt with can be a useful addition. The obstacle can be minor – a mobile phone that doesn't work or a delay to a train journey, or it might be something as simple as our investigator not having the witness's exact address, so that they have to ask around the neighbourhood in order to locate them. If the investigator is a policeman and the neighbourhood is dominated by a criminal gang, then we can introduce danger. If the witness is deaf or unable to speak the same language as the investigator, this is also a practical problem that has to be addressed.

More substantial obstacles, such as an accidental injury to the investigator or the coincidental death of the witness, might have a significance for the entire novel, and so the obstacle continues be an issue for some time. If Harry and Sally needed to reach the other side of the island in order to prevent the slimy lawyer escaping, and the only road were to have been destroyed by the hurricane making that journey very difficult, then overcoming this challenge and completing the journey could take several scenes, as well as presenting opportunities to introduce conflict and physical danger.

A **subtext** to a scene is another ingredient worth considering. What you're looking for here is something that is going on underneath the surface – an element that might be hidden, or at least obscured, from the reader or from the storytelling character and which may undermine what is ostensibly happening in the scene, giving it a more complex or perhaps even completely different meaning when the subtext is revealed. When you reveal the subtext is dictated by how you want to tell your story. Often you will reveal what is really going on underneath the surface later in the scene or very shortly afterwards, but sometimes it is better to let the subtext run through multiple scenes, with the revelation coming later in the novel as a twist that is a surprise to many of the characters and, indeed, the reader. It is also possible to reveal the subtext before the start of the scene where the reader is aware of the hidden element and its implications, although not all of the characters involved may be.

All of that can require some explanation so let's go back to our murder mystery and consider a scene where the investigator goes to a colleague's house for dinner. On arrival, the investigator realises that the colleague's wife is an ex-lover, a fact which neither he nor the wife wants the colleague to become aware of. In this scene, you could immediately reveal the nature of the investigator's dilemma to the reader, which will allow them to understand and observe the character's awkwardness. Alternatively, you could merely hint to the reader that there is some kind of history between the characters through how the scene is written but keep the reader, and the colleague, in the dark as to exactly what it is. Once you have decided that this previous relationship exists, whether you reveal it to the reader or not, any subsequent scene involving these characters is going to have an underlying tension. You could also introduce another subtext in that the investigator discovers he is still in love with the wife but, out of loyalty to his colleague, decides to show no sign of it to either the wife or, of course, the colleague. You could even go further and decide that the colleague knows about the past relationship and this knowledge, when it comes to light, will place the relationship between the investigator and the colleague that has existed throughout the novel in a new light but will also have shaped that relationship, depending on the colleague's attitude to the knowledge. Indeed, if you wanted to complicate things a little more still, you might decide that the colleague knows that he has a terminal illness throughout the story, but heroically hides it from his wife and the investigator in the hopes that they will reignite their old relationship, although that might be going a little too far. Even for me.

The key point however is that your knowledge of what the characters are keeping secret will colour how you write the scenes between them. The reader may not know that the characters were lovers in the past but your knowledge will necessarily change the way the characters interact. No matter how careful you are, your efforts to make sure the characters behave logically in overall story terms will be visible to the reader. They may not know *what* is going on underneath the surface of the scene, but they'll be aware that *something* is going on. Once alerted, the reader will hopefully try to work out what the subtext might be and, therefore, be engaged.

If the reader is aware that a character has a secret and what it is, the tension and complexity can still derive from the fact that another character in the scene is not aware of it. If we go back to *Hurricane*, Sally may presume Harry is romantically available, up until the point she sees him hugging an attractive woman on the beach. Both Harry and Sally will have information in a subsequent scene that the other doesn't – Harry that the woman is his sister and Sally that she has seen Harry hugging a beautiful woman on the sand. The reader can have both pieces of information and still be engaged by the scene, wondering how Harry and Sally will get themselves out of the mess, and entertained by how Harry and Sally may well make the situation even worse before they do. If we have a straightforward information-gathering scene in our mystery novel, where the investigator is interviewing a suspect of the opposite sex, then introducing a strong, but hidden, attraction between them – or, even better, a strong, but hidden, antipathy – this will alter how the scene develops. If one of the characters is unaware of the emotion on the other side, it's going to change the shape of the scene still further.

On the wider structural level, having something going on underneath the surface of the novel can lead to a twist or reveal towards the end of the novel which changes everything the characters, and the reader, have understood up to that point. This can be a very satisfying development in the novel, if used cautiously.

Who is in control of the scene?

If you identify which character is in control at the beginning of a scene, then you will often find that there is a potential shift in control to another character over its course, and a struggle for control that can make the scene much more interesting for the reader. Control is clearly connected to the conflict in the scene, so it's worth considering separately.

Defining 'control' for these purposes is difficult as it's often as much about the ability to decide how the scene proceeds, as it is about physical or practical control. If we take the murder mystery as an example, our investigator might be interviewing a reluctant witness in a police station, which means that our investigator is in physical and practical control of the scene, particularly if the witness has been arrested. If the witness starts the scene not having revealed the needed information (his objective) and the interviewer still has not succeeded in getting that information (his objective) then, to an extent, the witness is in actual control, at least temporarily. The interviewer's practical control (over how the interview will go forward) is clearly an advantage however and the witness will need to disrupt this. If the witness were an attractive woman, for example, they might flirt with the investigator in the hopes of distracting them. Similarly, a politically well-connected witness might threaten the investigator or demand to see their superior. If the witness manages to avoid answering the questions until the end of the scene, they will have succeeded in retaining actual control and have achieved their objective of not divulging the information. However, the scene will likely work better in terms of the overall story if the investigator, who is our central character after all, succeeds in persuading the witness to talk. In order to do this, they may have to threaten, cajole, reassure, trick or adopt some other strategy. From our perspective, identifying the conflicting objectives and where the control lies will allow us to think more clearly about the struggle between the characters, a shift in control over the course of the scene and how we might structure that shift so that it works from a story point of view.

The mystery novel example is fairly straightforward but let's consider an example in *Hurricane*. Perhaps Harry and his environmentally conscious friends on the island are set to have a meeting with Sally, her father, the slimy lawyer Ricky, and the developers behind the proposed marina. Harry's objective in this scene might well be two-fold, firstly to persuade the developers to place the marina elsewhere and secondly, as always, to improve his relationship with Sally. Ricky, on the other hand, is probably going to seek to avoid any meaningful discussion or negotiation, and to try to make Harry less attractive to Sally. If he is chairing and therefore controlling the meeting, he will have an advantage. However, for our scene to work in story terms, Harry needs to make his point and also to impress Sally at the same time. We could allow Harry to seize control of the agenda, perhaps by revealing Ricky's duplicity in some way, or Sally could intervene to ensure Harry is allowed to present his case (at which task he will excel), or one of the other characters present could change the course of the meeting in some way to give Harry more control over its direction. Whichever approach we take, we're thinking about control as a framework for the conflict in the scene and using control to structure the narrative. It's not going to give us all the answers, but it's a revealing perspective to take.

In summary, thinking about the characters' objectives, the situation at the beginning and end of a scene and the shift in control between those two points should help us to structure the scene in a way that will, hopefully, be helpful.

When to end a scene

Each scene in your novel is probably going to have at least one narrative purpose (and, if it doesn't, it probably should). If you know the narrative purpose of the scene, it probably goes without saying that you should end it soon after you have achieved it. Of course, the scene can have more than one purpose, but the same principle applies – if you continue a scene after they have been attained, then you probably need to have a good reason to do so. Anything that is superfluous to the purpose of the scene can slow down or distract from the story. In general, then, although there will always be exceptions, end as soon as you are able to and you probably won't go too far wrong.

How to end a scene

Momentum in a novel comes, at least partially, from regularly engaging the reader's interest. Often this is done by posing a question that they want answered or encouraging them to read on in the expectation of some upcoming event or revelation. When you are looking to end a scene (or indeed a chapter), be aware that it's a great place to engage the reader. If you present them with a hook of some kind, then that can lead very naturally to the next scene and create a sense of anticipation at the same time. It can be seem a little contrived to try and hook the reader at the end of every scene (but it's certainly something you can consider).

Let's think about questions first. One way to place a question in the reader's mind is for the point-of-view character (the character 'telling' the scene) to ask themself it in their internal monologue. For example, if a key event or an interesting revelation has occurred in the scene, then the storytelling character might draw attention to its significance and ask themselves whether the revelation or event will create a new challenge for the central character or consider how it will affect what might happen in the next scene. An example in the murder mystery novel would be the investigator being told that a suspect is well-acquainted with a known criminal. The investigator may not understand what the acquaintance signifies at that moment, but they could ask what it means and perhaps think of a strategy for uncovering its significance. If the point-of-view character is considering such a question, then the reader will be as well. Indeed, the point of view character may not know as much as the reader, and their suppositions may be incorrect, which will hopefully add another element to the reader's interest.

Be aware that if you set out a question for the reader, then you also implicitly promise that the question will be answered or dealt with in some way. For example, if Harry uncovers something unflattering about the slimy lawyer and asks himself what Sally would make of this information, then you probably have to make sure that the reader finds out Sally's reaction quite soon afterwards.

Another way to create a question in the reader's mind is through action or observation. For example, once a scene's purpose has been achieved, you might have the point-of-view character notice the presence of a mysterious man lurking outside the central character's home. You could withhold the mysterious man's identity from the reader, but indicate the point-of-view character knows who they are and that their presence is a threat. By withholding the man's identity and mentioning the threat, you will be encouraging the reader to speculate as to who the man might be and also wonder what threat they may pose. Aside from encouraging the reader to read on, telling the reader about the man and the threat can be useful for the next scene – particularly if the central character is unaware of the threat. Because the reader knows about a threat that the central character doesn't, the reader will be concerned for their wellbeing and anticipating an imminent danger which the central character will have to overcome. In other words, the reader will be engaged.

Another approach would be to have the point-of-view character give the mysterious man's identity to the reader, but not be aware of his significance and the threat that the man represents. Here, the reader knows the mystery man's presence represents a danger to the central character even if the other characters do not and will be asking themselves what the mystery man will do and how will the central character react.

You could even switch the point of view at the end of the scene to that of the mysterious man. In this case, the mysterious man's perspective will reveal to the reader their intentions, good or bad, towards the central character. You might also be able to reveal key information which the mysterious man has, but the central character doesn't, and which will almost certainly have implications for the central character in the upcoming part of the story. Again, this puts the reader at an advantage over the central character, in that they know something that the central character doesn't, creating anticipation in the mind of the reader as well as questions.

You don't need to have a hook or a question to encourage the reader to look forward to the next scene, however. Even something as simple as telling the reader where the next scene is set can help build a sense of anticipation, as will informing them that certain characters will soon be present in the story.

Summary

Writing is not an exact art; therefore, it is difficult to distil everything into a single ingredients list. Adding a dash of drama, or a pinch of pathos into your work occasionally would be a good suggestion. As I introduced on pages 156–62, conflict, risk, obstacles and subtext can all add additional flavour to your scenes, but you as the author will need to make the judgement as to what needs adding, what needs cutting back and when the scene is 'just right'.

If you are in need of a starting point, think about the five W's: Where, When, Who, What and Why.

- **Where** is the scene taking place?
- **When** is the scene taking place in the storyline? And **when** will the scene start?
- **Who** is the POV character? And **who** will they interact with?
- **What** is the object or the goal of this scene? And **what** happens in the scene?
- **Why** is this scene relevant to the overall storyline?

These simple questions may seem obvious, but simple questions are easy to remember, and therefore easy for you as a writer to consider as you plot, plan and write your scenes.

CHAPTER 8

Dialogue

As we've established, a novel consists of a series of events and interactions, chosen and arranged by the author to make a story – ideally with a beginning, a middle and an end. What keeps the story moving forward is often new information. New information creates challenges and obstacles, suggests ways to overcome them, tells us about the characters and changes relationships and, your story is probably going to be shaped, to a large extent, by the information that the characters, particularly the central character, acquire through dialogue.

The purpose of dialogue

Each piece of dialogue needs to have a storytelling purpose as well as, ideally, contributing to the reader's enjoyment of your novel. So, what kind of dialogue will earn its place and what kind of dialogue might you be better off avoiding?

- **Dialogue that introduces the novel's characters to the reader, and to each other.** If your novel is going to involve a romance, then it is going to be essential that the potential lovers meet. Using the example of our novel *Hurricane*, if Harry is going to achieve his objective of being in a long-term relationship with Sally, they will each have to find things about the other that appeal to them. You may use the POV character's internal thoughts and what they notice about the physical appearance and actions of the other characters but much of the useful information will probably be revealed through what the characters say to each other, how they say it and, occasionally, what they *don't* say.

- **Dialogue that reveals the characters' personalities and key information about them**. It's unlikely you will be able to, or want to, reveal everything about a character's personality when they first appear in the novel, although you will probably give a strong indication. The subsequent meetings involving the character will develop the reader's initial impressions and shape their understanding of them as an individual. Whereas the reader's first encounter with her might reveal Sally to be attractive, intelligent and witty, subsequent meetings may give important information about her likes and dislikes, her past, her aspirations for her future and all the other information and insights that will be essential to create a rounded character.
- **Dialogue that reveals information about how the characters feel about each other.** Aside from showing aspects of each character's personality, you will also need to show how they feel about the other characters in the novel. If Sally is in a relationship with Ricky, the slimy lawyer, then the health (or otherwise) of that relationship will be reflected by how they talk to each other, but also by how they talk to other characters *about* each other. As the relationship changes over the course of the novel, Sally's concerns and changing affections would probably be revealed through a series of conversations; in each of which, her declining affection for Ricky will probably be reflected in the words you give her. You may also use her internal thoughts about the relationship, but if their relationship is deteriorating it will probably do so, at least partially, through a series of escalating confrontations.
- **Dialogue that reveals information about a character's motivations**. Showing the conflicting motivations of the characters will be important for any novel. Your novel will

struggle to achieve forward momentum if the characters want the same thing. If they do want the same thing, they will need to want to achieve them using different methods. One of the key moments in the break-down of Sally's relationship with Ricky might be her uncovering his true motivations both in their relationship and in the wider story. That discovery may well come through a conversation between him and Sally, or through Sally being told the truth by another character. Even if she finds out about his nefarious plans through an email or some scenario that doesn't involve dialogue per se, she will still discuss her discovery with other characters in order to make sense of it. Of course, you may wish to tell the reader about Ricky's true intentions earlier in the novel. If the reader knows about his duplicity before Sally does, this will lead to tension – again, a conversation between the lawyer and one of his co-conspirators may be the easiest way to do this. Similar explanatory conversations will happen elsewhere in the novel, in one form or another – either with Sally discovering or revealing information, or with other characters revealing it to the reader only. Sally will also need to understand that Harry's motivations generally, and particularly towards her, are well intentioned and this will probably emerge from direct conversations *and* what she discovers about him from other characters. If her father alters his aim from wanting to protect Sally from Harry to something more positive, the change will probably come through or as a result of a discussion.

- **Dialogue that reveals key plot information.** As we know, a tropical storm is heading the way of the characters in *Hurricane*, and it will probably be announced by a character speaking directly or through a radio report. Similarly, explaining to the reader the dangers that a marina will pose to the island's marine life will probably be done most successfully through a conversation.

- **Dialogue describing significant events where a POV character can't be present.** Although telling action through dialogue is never an ideal solution to a storytelling problem, sometimes it is your only choice. If Ricky meets with a dubious contact and is given a fat envelope either Ricky, or the dubious character or a watcher could tell the reader about it through their storytelling POV. However, if you were only using Harry and Sally's storytelling POVs, this would not be possible and a conversation where the watcher tells Sally what he saw would be necessary.
- **Dialogue that misleads the reader and/or the characters.** Often you will want to misdirect the reader, and the characters, either through a character giving misinformation or misleading another character. This will almost always be done through dialogue. Misinformation and misunderstandings work as obstacles in a novel, creating a problem that can generally only be solved by uncovering the truth. If, for example, Sally's sister tells her that Harry is married then until the reality of the matter is revealed, Sally will not be willing to become romantically involved with him.

As dialogue will probably play a major role in your novel , you will need to ensure each exchange is as effective as possible. In order to achieve this aim, identify the exchange's purpose (or perhaps purposes) and focus the conversation on that. A conversation in real life may take two hours but in fiction you need to be much more efficient, so you'll want to boil the exchange down to a few pages, if not a couple of paragraphs. If you know the purpose of the exchange, you can generally dispense with much of the conversation that isn't directly related to it but you may have a series of purposes you want to achieve. If, for example, you want Sally to end her relationship with Ricky the lawyer, then that will be one aim of the exchange. You may, however, also want to give his reaction to the split. There may be still other elements that you will want to include in the conversation for story reasons. If you want to show that the conversation is difficult for Sally, then starting the exchange earlier might give you the opportunity to show her hesitation and efforts to minimise her decision's impact. Indeed, if you have established Sally as a kind and caring person then you will probably want the exchange to show a consistent version of the personality that you have shown up to that point. The conversation may also have several plot purposes: aside from terminating the relationship between them, it could also reveal other information, perhaps relevant to the mutual attraction between Harry and Sally, or show that she knows that the lawyer has misled her.

Control

Once you have identified the purpose of a piece of dialogue and written your first version of the conversation, it is worth considering how you might be able to improve it. One element always worth considering is who starts the conversation in control and whether that control changes as the conversation proceeds. Let's take a conversation between Sally and her father as an example. It may well be that the father assumes a dominant role in the conversation because of his parental position and, without thinking about it, he may define the terms of the conversation in various ways. For example, he may have an expectation that Sally will treat his opinions with respect and agree with them. He may also expect Sally will behave politely and display what he perceives as good behaviour. There may be topics which he will not want to discuss, such as Sally's sexual attraction to Harry, and ones he refuses to discuss, such as his own bad behaviour. For your purposes, as a writer, having a character in actual or perceived control of the conversation as a starting point is useful because it gives you the opportunity to shift the control of the conversation to another character by the end of the scene. If Sally pushes back and breaks the rules that her father imposes, this could be an important shift in their relationship allowing her to obtain the independence she will need to achieve her objective in the novel (being in a happy relationship with Harry). Each conversation with her father may therefore be a stage in achieving something like equality – or at least an acceptance of each other as individuals with free will.

Almost every conversation, in fiction and in real life, can be looked at through the prism of control. A discussion between an employer and an employee will probably favour the employer. If a police officer is interviewing a suspect, the police officer will probably be the one deciding which questions should be asked, and answered. With this in mind, it is worth asking yourself some questions when considering a fictional conversation.

Who initiates the conversation?

Often the character who initiates an exchange knows what they want to achieve and this puts them at an advantage. If Sally initiates a conversation in which she wants to talk to her father about a problem with his business, she will be aware that he may be reluctant to discuss the matter with her. As a result, she will need to have a strategy to persuade him to engage with her on the topic. She might well start with a round-about approach, raising the issue with a seemingly innocent question. If, for example, she is aware that her father has had an unfortunate argument with an important client, she might approach the matter with a question about where he was the night before, knowing that was when the argument took place. Her father is more likely to respond to an indirect approach, bearing in mind the historical imbalance that often exists in parent–child relationships. He may not, initially at least, be aware that she knows all about the evening and that it ended with her father behaving badly. Alternatively, she may present the results of the argument immediately, telling him that an important contract has been cancelled. By taking this head-on approach and presenting the situation as a problem that needs to be addressed, she may be hoping that her father will see the issue as a business problem rather than a personal one.

Who sets the terms of the conversation?

Generally, the participant with an accepted position of authority or dominance over the other participants in any exchange is the one who will decide how it will proceed, or if it should proceed at all. In our example of a conversation between Sally and her father, he will probably expect to control the subject matter. If Sally wants to talk to him about an aspect of his business, he may well want to limit the scope of it and the questions which she can ask. On the other hand, if he wants to talk to Sally about her romance with Harry, then he may well expect her to listen to what he has to say even if she finds his comments intrusive and unwelcome. The control of the exchange may also extend to how he expects Sally to talk to him. He might have very little tolerance for her challenging him and be displeased if she gives advice, no matter how good, on his business activities or personal life, even though he feels no such restrictions when it comes to her private life and career. As mentioned before, Sally's father could also impose restrictions as to the way in which the conversation takes place revolving around behaviour, deference and gravity – all of which Sally might resist.

You will probably see a similar control dynamic in conversations between senior officers and the soldiers serving under them, teachers and their students, and priests and members of their congregation. In these situations the control is fairly straightforward but sometimes the control can be more subtle or manipulative. If Harry and Sally are going on their first date, Harry may adapt how he behaves so that he appears more appealing to her, perhaps relinquishing control to her, or being instead more assertive than he normally would be. By way of contrast, Ricky may exert control in his conversations with Sally by questioning her judgement, undermining her opinions or not paying any attention to what she has to say.

Will the other participant in the conversation resist the control?

Once you have identified that a participant has control over the conversation, then the question is whether that will persist until the end of the conversation. For example, Sally may decide it is time to stand up to her father and force him to have a conversation where topics he would rather not address are discussed on a more equal basis. If she does not succeed with charm, she may resort to persuasion of a different kind – perhaps offering him an inducement of some kind, or threatening to no longer work for him or even to leave the island. It could turn out that her father's position is not as secure as he thinks it is but, by the same measure, he may also have threats, inducements and other emotional pressures that he can bring to bear.

The resistance to the original control will come in different ways. For example, if a female detective is interviewing a violent criminal in his house, he is almost certain not to want to talk about the crime that she is investigating. She may attempt to persuade him to talk by threatening him with a search of the house or charges relating to another matter but he could try to disrupt her focus by flirting with her. His strategy is essentially one of distraction but it might be effective, combined as it is with the implicit threat his violent record implies.

If there is a shift in control, how might that change the conversation (and the direction) of your story?

Because there will be a limited number of scenes in your novel – sometimes fewer than a hundred, often not much more – then each scene will have to help the story in a significant way. Scenes in which the relationships between your characters change, whether in the balance between them, the way they feel about each other, or the way in which they will co-exist, are obviously going to be key moments in any story. Indeed, much of *Hurricane*'s story will revolve around the changes in the relationships between the characters. Whereas Harry and Sally might be in opposition to each other at the beginning of the story, they will inevitably come to see each other in a much more positive light by the end. While Sally's father may be a domineering, if loving, parent at the start of the novel, his relationship with Sally will be more equal by the end. Sally's unsatisfactory relationship with Ricky will also change from one where he is in control to one where he has been completely discarded. These changes will be reflected in a series of exchanges, most of which will involve dialogue. The characters will express their feelings to each other, stand up for themselves or, alternatively, attempt to dominate each other. With each of these moments, considering how the balance of power in the conversation shifts will help make the scene more dramatic and more interesting for the reader. The control in a conversation, and in a relationship, may switch back and forth. If, for example, Ricky suspects that Sally has been cheating on him with Harry, then he may start the conversation with some degree of moral superiority. Even if Sally is innocent of any physical indiscretion, she may well feel guilty about her growing feelings for Harry. If, however, the lawyer overplays his hand, perhaps forbidding her to see Harry again, she may rightly resent this and the balance may shift again. If, as the conversation becomes more heated, Ricky inadvertently reveals that he has done something underhand concerning Harry, then it will shift once more. The basic purpose of the scene is to show Sally's estrangement from the lawyer but introducing complexities based around control is going to help the scene become more interesting and engaging for the reader.

Motivation

Another element to consider when approaching an exchange of dialogue is what each of the participants want to achieve – and sometimes avoid – in a scene. I like to think of my characters as actors asking me to give them notes to help with their performance. If I know what each character's motivation is in the exchange, then I can, if needed, tweak it to ensure that there are points of conflict which will give the scene more energy. Not every piece of dialogue needs a clash of motivations, of course, but when you're writing a novel you are often looking for ways in which to enhance even the most transactional of conversations. For example, John may run into Jack in a newsagent with the sole purpose of establishing that Jack was there rather than somewhere else. If you introduce another element, however, such as Jack's embarrassment at being observed buying an explicit magazine, or John's sudden attraction to Jack, then the scene acquires a more interesting angle that could engage the reader more effectively.

Here are some straightforward questions that can help ensure that you have the motivations worked out in advance. It's often surprising how helpful these questions can be.

What do the characters hope to achieve from the exchange and how do they plan to achieve it?

This is an essential question to ask about any exchange between characters where you want to ensure that there is some momentum in the scene. If the characters have the same agendas, there is a danger that the scene will be flat. If they want different things from the scene, and have conflicting strategies as to how to obtain their intended aims, then you will almost certainly have some added spark to it. If, for example, Harry meets Sally to discuss the marina that her father's company intends to build, his intention will be to persuade her of the uniqueness of the coral reef which the development will threaten. He may decide the best way to do this is by taking her diving on the reef, and he plans to relax her by ensuring she really enjoys herself. Sally, on the other hand, will want to keep the meeting professional, will claim to know all about the reef, having been snorkelling on it since she was a child, and will instead seek to show Harry how the development will not damage it but instead will open it up to sustainable tourism which will benefit the island as a whole. Naturally, their motivations will not be limited solely to the discussion of the marina. They may both be aware of their growing attraction for the other, but while Harry may see the meeting as an opportunity to turn that attraction into something more, Sally may want to avoid this at all costs. Identifying their motivations and placing them in opposition has helped us to create a framework for a scene that will tell us about the marina, the reef and the relationship between Harry and Sally in an entertaining way.

If the characters' motivations are in opposition, what effect will this have?

Giving the characters opposing motivations in an exchange is likely to lead to conflict, which will probably make the dialogue more dramatically engaging, but it may also suggest that you alter the character's behaviour. If a character is concerned, for example, that another character might be about to uncover an embarrassing secret then, rather than being passive, that character may well use deception, misdirection or bluster to avoid their secret being revealed. If a character's motivation is to appeal to the other character romantically, then they may use charm, flirtation and flattery to further their intentions. The other character will probably have stratagems of their own to ensure that the exchange goes the way they would prefer it to.

Do the characters' motivations change over the course of the exchange?

Many of the dialogue exchanges on your novel will provide new information to one or more of the participants, often changing their understanding of the situation that faces them. With the new perspective, it could be that a motivation they may have had at the beginning of the conversation alters, or is no longer applicable to them. If, for example, Harry meets Sally in a café with the intention of asking her out on a date his plans may shift if, in the course of the conversation, she mentions her boyfriend. His motivation, to make himself appealing to her with a view to a romantic relationship, may stay the same but it might be affected by the knowledge that Sally has given him. Similarly, Ricky may get on well with Harry until Harry lets slip his attraction to Sally, at which point Ricky's feelings towards Harry may change to something quite different.

Does a character have more than one motivation in a conversation?

Like people in real life, characters are often driven by more than one desire, sometimes conflicting, and these will make their approach to the conversation more nuanced. An example we have already mentioned elsewhere is when Sally and Harry are attracted to each other but find themselves in opposition over the development of the marina. Another example might be Harry having been invited for dinner in Sally's apartment but finding that he is allergic to her cat. On the one hand, Harry doesn't want to have a serious allergic reaction; on the other, he really wants to spend the evening with Sally. Harry might try to hide his allergic reaction in order not to spoil the opportunity to get to know Sally better, or suggest that they go for a walk on the beach instead.

Compromise

In some conversations, one participant will achieve their aim and another will not. For example, if a detective is questioning a suspect, they will succeed if they persuade the suspect to admit to the crime, whereas the suspect will have failed if they confess. The scene, if looked at slightly differently, may end with both parties achieving what they have set out to do – the detective getting their confession but the suspect keeping secret their involvement in a far greater crime. In another version, neither of the participants will achieve their aim entirely, but the detective may acquire useful information and the suspect will have presented an alibi, even if it isn't believed. All of these possible outcomes feature the participants maintaining their aim and motivation in the conversation. However, there is another alternative, which is that the characters adapt their aims over the course of the dialogue and, while being consistent with their original motivation, reach some sort of compromise. In this scenario, there may be proposals and counter proposals, a sharing of information designed to clarify positions, explanation of misunderstandings and other forms of negotiation aimed at achieving a mutually acceptable way forward. In *Hurricane*, the main characters will, at some stage, achieve a compromise that allows the marina to go ahead in a way that does not impact on the coral reef. The compromise will also allow Harry and Sally to achieve their more important motivation which is to be together romantically.

Is something going on underneath the surface of the conversation?

It's often a good idea to think of a conversation as being made up of two parts – that which is said and that which is unsaid. Sometimes that which is unspoken is the best dialogue, strange as that may sound. If Sally's lawyer boyfriend ask her if she loves him, her failure to reply may be the most effective answer of all. When approaching a piece of dialogue, it is worth asking yourself if there is a hidden layer to the conversation. For example, if two detectives are interviewing a female suspect with whom the male detective has had a previous relationship which must be kept secret from his colleague, you have an opportunity to create an exchange which has an interesting, but concealed, dynamic that reveals itself only to the reader. If the reader is unaware of the detective's dilemma, however, they will not appreciate his awkwardness and concern, or the tension that the risk of the relationship being uncovered will give rise to.

Often these exchanges with a hidden layer work best when there is a disconnect between the surface conversation and what is happening underneath. If two secret lovers meet in a social situation where it is vital their romance doesn't come to light, it doesn't mean that they won't want to communicate or pay close attention to each other's every gesture and hesitation to see if it contains a meaning intended solely for them. On the surface, they may be talking about the weather at a friend's Sunday barbeque, but underneath it may be a very different story.

One other element that you might want to consider inserting into the hidden part of a conversation is strong emotion. If one of the characters is concealing grief, happiness, love, hate or some other profound feeling, then it will affect how they interact with the other characters in the scene. Occasionally that emotion may be directed at another character. Harry may feel forced to conceal a strong dislike of one of Sally's acquaintances in a social interaction at which they are both present. Sally may be doing her best to hide her growing dislike of her current boyfriend.

Who is talking? and how?

Try to ensure that each important character has a distinctive 'voice' in your novel. The voice, or way that they speak, will often be an extension of their personality, but it will also be affected by their place of upbringing, their social class, their education and their employment. As discussed in Chapter 5, it is useful to ensure that your characters are different from each other. The differences may be in terms of personality, beliefs or emotional state, or could relate to their status or some other factor such as education or background. All of these provide points of conflict that will not only be important for your story, but also allow your characters to *speak differently* as well.

For example, if Harry is from Edinburgh but Sally grew up largely on a small Caribbean island, they will probably have very different accents and use different words for the same objects. Sally may see a truck whereas Harry would see a lorry. It's generally best to write accents neutrally on the page as opposed to writing them phonetically – 'I've come tae talk tae ye aboot the marina' will probably be less easily understood by the reader than 'I've come to talk to you about the marina', but once you have decided on a distinct accent for a character you can generally choose words and sentence constructions that suggest to the reader a way of speaking. In addition, you can occasionally remind the reader of accents that are not written down ('Harry's Scottish accent seemed more pronounced this evening'). It's also wise to be avoid using random words from another language to denote someone's nationality or heritage. Having a Frenchman call everyone he meets 'monsieur' can seem a little clunky, but that doesn't mean you can't suggest his accent in the choice of words he uses and allow him to draw attention to his nationality ('In France, food like this is not eaten. Not by humans, at least.')

The words a character uses in conversation may be a reflection of their education, position in society or the job they do. For example, an academic might 'hypothesise' but a baker probably wouldn't. On the other hand, sometimes playing around with expectations of how people should speak can create interesting character voices. If a gangster 'hypothesises', it might work very well. Bear in mind also that certain jobs have specialised language: policemen and pathologists have jargon that can be researched and used to create authenticity.

Characters also speak differently in different situations. For example, Harry might express himself one way at an employment interview and another way with some friends on the beach and another way again with Sally. He will also be affected by what is going on around him in the scene. If he is in danger, his way of speaking will probably be informed by that, as it would be if the scene is very romantic. Relationships also affect how characters speak. Harry will speak in a different way to Sally than he will to her father.

HOW DO YOUR CHARACTERS INTERACT?

One of the most important elements of good dialogue is that the characters listen to each other and that there is a logical connection between what is said in a conversation and what happens next. If a character says something that requires a reaction, then make sure the other participants in the conversation do so, even if their reaction is to deliberately ignore what has been said or to change the subject.

If a key piece of information is given, then it should be discussed or acted on.

It's absolutely crucial that the characters speak in a credible way. Occasionally you may be tempted to use dialogue to convey information about the setting or the characters that probably should be dealt with by the narrating prose. For example, if two characters are walking through a village in which they have both grown up, they will be unlikely to say 'Look Gerald, there is the fifteenth-century church of St Mary, in which you will be married next week to Deidre, the second daughter of the local butcher'. All of that information may be important but the conversation sounds false and you will have to think of a different way to convey it.

Writing dialogue is often a balancing act – you probably want to avoid your characters speaking in perfectly formed sentences, but you don't want them to be too natural either, as the hesitations, half-finished sentences and 'ums' and 'ahs' that make up most real life conversations can seem awkward on the page. Your dialogue needs to sound right to the ear but you also want it to be focussed on the purpose of the conversation. If your characters are too polite or become so loquacious that they don't get to the point, the dialogue can seem as though it is treading water. This is often because the exchanges in question, while acceptable in real life, have no narrative purpose in a novel and therefore no real importance to the reader, who will probably skip forward until they find something that has.

Carrying dialogue

Even the most brilliant dialogue needs prose around it to tell us who is saying what and how they are saying it. When telling the reader who is speaking, it is sensible to use neutral, almost invisible words. 'Said' is safest but 'answered', 'replied' and 'spoke in a low voice' all work well. Tread lightly, however, with dialogue-carrying verbs such as 'blurted', 'giggled' or 'squealed'; the intention is to describe the dialogue or convey the emotion behind it, but these verbs are often unnecessary as the context or the dialogue itself suggests the way the words are spoken. If your draft dialogue doesn't do that, however, then consider whether your description of the character's emotional state or the context give the reader sufficient information. That said, the occasional active dialogue-carrying verb is probably going to be okay. For example, 'he screamed' may be the most effective way of describing a particular piece of dialogue. Overuse of active dialogue-carrying verbs can be very visible in a novel and seldom improves it. For example:

'Isn't this the best news?' Jack giggled.
'I'm not sure it is,' Tom groaned.
'What do you mean?' Jack blurted.

As you can see, it can soon become quite visible.

Another habit authors can fall into when writing in dialogue, is putting the verb before the speaker. For example:

'Isn't this the best news?' said Jack.
'I'm not sure it is,' said Tom.
'What do you mean?' said Jack.

Again it can become quite visible and because it's an antiquated verb structure – you would very seldom use it when speaking naturally – it is best avoided. It is however, surprisingly common so perhaps this is my own personal bugbear.

Using adverbs repeatedly to carry dialogue is something else about which to be cautious. 'He said delightedly' is fine once in a while, but repeated use of this grammatical structure creates a pattern that can seem clumsy. For example:

'Isn't this the best news?' Jack said deliriously.
'I'm not sure it is,' Tom replied sombrely.
'What do you mean?' Jack said worriedly.

You can also use action or description to carry dialogue. For example:

'Isn't this the best news?' Jack smiled, rubbing his hands together.
'I'm not sure it is,' Tom shrugged, a frown creasing his forehead.
Jack turned to him, his concern apparent.
'What do you mean?'

It gives us a little more information about the characters, while the descriptions give the words a little more weight. Describing the character's movement may also help give the dialogue momentum.

Sometimes, of course, you don't need any prose to describe the dialogue, particularly in two-handed conversations that go back and forth and are fairly straightforward as to their meaning.

'Isn't this the best news?' Jack said.
'I'm not sure it is,' Tom replied.
'What do you mean?'

Once we have established that Jack and Tom are the only participants, then the reader will know who is speaking and when. It is sensible to remind the reader from time to time of the order, but if the conversation is unemotional and not complex then its best to use carrying language sparingly.

It is a different situation when the meaning behind the dialogue may not be immediately apparent to the reader. Here we can help them understand by allowing the narrating POV character to tell the reader what they are noticing about the other participant's demeanour and state of mind and, also, what they are thinking. For example:

'Isn't this the best news?' Jack said as he approached, his smile too shiny to be convincing. Tom wondered if Jack thought him a complete fool.
'I'm not sure it is,' Tom replied and he could hear the anger in his voice. So be it. He could tell from the alarm that passed over Jack's expression that he had noticed it too.

'What do you mean?' Jack said, and the alarm turned to fear when Tom took a step forward, lifting a finger to point at him.

Obviously, we are giving a lot more information to the reader here, but we need to. On the surface the dialogue is the same as before, but with the additional information it takes on a completely different significance. Giving this kind of detail about the characters is particularly important when the scenes are emotional or complex in some other way. For example, if Harry and Sally are walking on the beach after their first date, and Harry is the narrating POV, then he should probably be hyper-aware of Sally's emotional state and of his own. Conveying these emotions and the tension that goes with them is going to bring the scene to life for the reader. Similarly, if Jack and Tom are meeting for the first time after Tom has discovered that Jack has betrayed him then Jack, as the narrating POV, is going to be watching Tom very closely and picking up on any signs that will reveal his nervousness or duplicity. He will also be conveying to the reader his own anger and suspicion.

Aside from the language describing the dialogue itself, also consider what might be going on in the background to see if you can insert something that will give some weight to the dialogue or enhance it in some other way. For example, if Harry and Sally are walking on the beach, there might be moonlight and softly lapping waves; there is always a danger of stepping over into cliché, which you might be tempted to make use of.

Another aspect to be aware of is that very long speeches can be difficult to read so consider breaking them up with action, description or questions from another participant. Dialogue works best when there are two active participants, so if one is doing all the talking then at least make sure we are aware of the listener's reactions to what is being said.

One last point with regard to dialogue is that I always start new dialogue on a new line and give any reaction on a new line as well. I also put the dialogue first so that it is visible to the reader. Readers sometimes skip over descriptive passages but they seldom skip over dialogue as it's where a lot of important information is given. An example would be this passage:

Jack took Tom's elbow and whispered 'I'm right behind you' in his ear.
'I know you are,' Tom said.

I would probably rewrite it like this:

Jack took Tom's elbow and whispered in his ear.
'I'm right behind you.'
'I know you are,' Tom said.

The decisions you make, however, as to how to write your own dialogue are entirely up to you. But if you think about why the dialogue is needed, what else might be happening round the conversation and how best to present it, then your choices will probably be the ones that work best for your novel.

Summary

To reiterate what was discussed in this chapter, look at the list of questions below. When you are writing, or even editing your dialogue, work through this list and mentally tick off the ones that apply. If your dialogue does not conform a least one of the points below, then it implies that the speech has little purpose. All dialogue must be relevant enough and push the story forward in order to make the final cut.

So, has your dialogue:

- created a challenge or obstacle for your central character/s to overcome?
- presented a way for the central character/s to overcome the challenge or obstacle they face?
- introduced a new character?

- developed a character, revealing more of their personality and possibly revealing their goal?
- revealed how your characters feel about one another?
- revealed character motivation?
- revealed a key plot point?
- described a significant event that the POV character was not privy to?
- provided misinformation, or misdirected the central character in a way that will create tension and an obstacle for the central character?

CHAPTER 9

You've finished your novel – what do you do now?

First and foremost – congratulations. It's been a long journey, no doubt made up of its fair share of backward steps, frustrations and diversions – but you have persevered and you have triumphed. Whatever happens after this point, you have achieved something remarkable that only other writers will ever really understand. Whether your novel is destined for the Booker Prize or only friends and family, it represents commitment and enthusiasm for your own creative process and a certain amount of toughness and endurance. Take a moment to pat yourself on the back. The good news is that you have put all that hard work in and you have something – your novel – to show for it. The bad news is you probably need to put in more work to see it achieve its full potential.

In other words, you have to see if you can get this novel published.

Is it really finished?

If you're going to send your novel out to agents or publishers, it needs to be as good as you can possibly make it. You generally only get one chance with an agent. If they reject it, they probably won't want to see the novel again unless they specifically ask you to resubmit after a rewrite – so you need to get your novel as close to perfect as possible before you send it out into the world. In order to make sure that's the case, even if you have done several rewrites and are pretty confident of its quality, you need to get an *objective* confirmation that your novel is ready for submission. This objective view should confirm that the story is soundly structured and commercial (in other words, that other people will want to read it), that the prose is tight and clear and that the characters are interesting and can carry the novel. In short, much of what we have been talking about in the previous chapters of this book.

If you belong to a good writers' group, and are regularly reading and criticising other writer's material, you may have acquired the ability to take a distanced, objective view on your own work already. If not, there are a few approaches you can take:

- **Put it in a drawer.** It may sound strange but if you want to discover the real state of your novel, not looking at it for a few months will often reveal its flaws and strengths. When you're too close to it, it's very difficult to see the mistakes and inconsistencies. When you have a little bit of distance, they become all too apparent.
- **Read it aloud.** Again, this may sound counter-intuitive but reading your novel to yourself out loud will often give you the distance you need to see it clearly. Try and read it in one or two sittings, if possible, and don't edit your script as you read – just highlight the places that need work. What you're trying to do is listen to your writing line-to-line, but also get an overview of the story. Reading it through in a focussed way will help with that. Hearing the sound of your words also highlights clumsy grammar, word repetitions, bad dialogue, mistakes with rhythm and all the other minor, but fixable, issues that it makes sense to address before submission.
- **Ask someone else to read it.** Ideally, this should be someone you trust to give you a constructive and realistic view. The kind of person you're looking for is probably not a close relative or partner who thinks that everything you do is wonderful. There needs to be a little bit of emotional distance. You also need to find someone who reads a lot and whose opinions on writing you respect. After all, if your reader doesn't read novels very often, their opinion may not be very useful. Finally, you need

to persuade them to be completely honest in their opinions, although perhaps not completely brutal. This kind of reader is not always easy to find but look around and, if you are lucky enough to find one, hold onto them. This will hopefully not be the only novel you write.

- **Find a freelance editor.** If none of the above options have worked as well as you hoped and you are still uncertain of your manuscript's condition, there is another option. This, however, is the option that you'll have to pay for, but given how much time and effort you've put into this novel of yours already, it may well be worth investing a little money as well. A good freelance editor should have experience editing fiction at a commercial publishing house or, alternatively, be a commercially published novelist. Several writing organisations and commercial ventures offer editing services, including Writers & Artists, and they vary widely in price and usefulness. If you are going to go down this route, ask around (perhaps online) to see who other aspiring writers would recommend. It's also sensible to get in contact with the editor or reader in advance to discuss exactly what you are looking for. Some reader reports, which some editors and writing organisations offer, can be very thin on detailed feedback when what you may well want is a line-by-line edit, as well as the more standard advice on characters and the structure. On the other hand, if you are happy with the quality of the prose, then you may be looking for more of an overview. Don't rush into making a decision - research your options, decide on your budget and do your best to get an independent view, whether by testimonial or otherwise, of the editor's suitability for your project.

Identifying which agents to submit to

It is still possible to submit to some publishers directly but these days the majority of the larger publishing houses only accept submissions via agents. That said, it is worth researching your market – specialist publishers for specific genres such as children's fiction may be more flexible, as might be smaller independent publishers. The good news is there are a lot of good agents who are keen to represent new authors. The bad news is that the odds are stacked against you if you are looking at one agent in particular. Most will receive well over a thousand submissions a year, from which they may take on only a handful. Even if you have written a brilliant novel, you may accumulate quite a few rejection letters before you are successful. However, each time you submit, your submission will be read (eventually) and it will be read by someone who is hoping that you are the new author they are looking for.

The *Writers' & Artists' Yearbook* has traditionally provided an up-to-date list of commercial agents in the UK and Ireland. Nearly all of these agents will have their own websites which will give further information about them and their authors. There are also other listing websites, including the Writers & Artists website, www.writersandartists.co.uk, which will provide addresses and contact details. A good source for recent deal information can be found in the *Bookseller*, the publishing industry's weekly magazine. You can sign up to its mailing list for free which will give you summaries of recent articles and will often mention particular agents, although more detail can be accessed only via its paywall-protected website

Another way to identify agents who you think might be a match for you is through festivals and writing organisations. Many of these organise events where aspiring writers can pitch their ideas to an agent, either in one-to-one sessions or in a more public format. Participating in a 'pitch an agent' event can provide useful feedback on the premise of your novel and sometimes also on an extract from it (depending on whether the agent sees that or not). In addition, there may also be an opportunity to meet the agent socially afterwards. If you get on with them, and they are even remotely encouraging, this may be an introduction you can follow up on when you are ready to submit.

Social media is also a very effective way to find out about agents and what they do. Many agents, particularly the younger ones, will have Twitter and Instagram accounts and some of them have blogs which they will occasionally link to. The better ones will offer helpful advice on how to submit and, sometimes, how not to submit. They will also give indications as to what kind of new fiction they and the market are looking for. If one of them expresses an interest in a type of novel which could describe yours, you have a useful way to approach them. If, over time, you have the occasional Twitter conversation, you may have another.

So, what kinds of agent are you looking for? Here are some suggestions that might be worth bearing in mind:

- **An agent with a good reputation.** The best way to establish an agent's reputation is by looking at the authors they represent. If their list includes top authors who have been with them for their entire careers, then the likelihood is that the agent has been at least partially responsible for their success and that their clients are happy with them. It also means the agent has a track record that editors in-house at publishing companies will be aware of. If an agent of this calibre submits a novel by a debut author to an editor, then the editor will probably put it to the top of the pile. A word of warning, though – agents usually operate separately. Even though Agent A and Agent B might be at the same agency, they can have very different reputations and have very different lists. One might represent high end literary novels and the other represent more commercial fiction. One might have 30 years' experience, while another might only have 3. Make sure you don't confuse who the agency represents and who an individual agent represents.
- **An agent who is looking for new clients.** Good agents can only represent a certain number of authors well and sometimes they reach capacity. Look on their website and if they say they are closed to new submissions, believe them.

- **An agent who is looking for novels like yours.** Many agents are generalists and represent a wide variety of writing, from non-fiction to fantasy and everything in between. Even so, many generalists list genres of novel that they are particularly looking for and also mention types of novel that they do not feel comfortable representing. If you look at an agency's website, you can also sometimes work out what kind of fiction a particular agent is drawn to from the novelists they represent. If your novel is likely to be categorised in a certain genre, such as crime or fantasy, there will be agents who specialise in that genre and they should probably be top of your list. Specialist agents know their market, and the editors that make support it, very well.
- **A younger agent who is building their list.** The top agencies are ongoing ventures and while the most respected agents will have very full lists and not much room or time for debut novelists, a younger agent with a smaller list may be more active and able to give you much more attention. They may also have good relationships with younger editors who are also building their own stables of authors. Look for younger agents with well-chosen clients who have done recent deals.
- **An agent with editorial experience**. There is a certain amount of career overlap between publishing houses and literary agencies. Your first novel can be very important for your career so if you can identify an agent who has either worked to a high level as an editor or who makes it clear that they work with their clients on their manuscripts before submitting, that is ideal, as it can mean that your novel will have a better chance of short and long term success.
- **Agents to avoid.** Finally, there will be agents you should exclude, either because they have few clients who they don't represent very well or because they have an agenda which is more about exploitation that representation. Anyone, for example, who

charges you to submit to them or charges for editorial feedback is probably not the kind of agent you want to represent you and may not in fact be a real agent at all. We'll talk a little bit later about how agents make their money, but their remuneration comes as a percentage of what they earn for you and very seldom in any other way. Similarly, an agent who operates on their own, has limited experience within the industry and doesn't represent any commercially published authors is probably a waste of your time. If they have not been successful representing their clients up to this point, it is unlikely they will be able to represent you successfully either.

Even if you use these criteria to try and focus your efforts, you may find you have a long list of potential agents to contact. This isn't necessarily a problem. When you submit, you should probably do so in stages, with the first round of submissions going to your top ten agents, the next round to another ten and so on. Although you may be lucky and achieve instant success, the likelihood is that you will have to submit over several rounds. You will also have to wait and be patient. Response times will be indicated on most agents' websites and they are often up to three months, or even longer. There is a good reason, however, why you should submit in batches. You can learn a certain amount from the responses you receive each time and adjust your approach for the next round.

If you're lucky, you may get a personalised letter from the agent telling you what they liked and disliked about your submission. This is excellent news, even if the novel isn't, ultimately, for them. A busy agent taking time to give you a considered view on your novel means that they see something in it. You should pay close attention to any advice or suggestions they offer as they probably know what they are talking about. If you're even luckier, they will ask you to resubmit after you have worked on some of their suggestions, or done a complete rewrite. This is a real opportunity that you should take every advantage of.

Another possibility is that, having read your submission, an agent will ask for a full script. They may still reject your novel but their asking for the complete novel tells you that your submission is attracting interest, although perhaps that the rest of the novel isn't at the same standard.

Even if all the agents you submit to reply with pro-forma rejection letters, you have still learned something – that unfortunately your submission package needs a little bit more work. There are very few writers who don't have a collection of rejection letters but remember that agents really do want to represent new authors with excellent novels. It's how they make a living.

How to submit to an agent

Firstly, and most importantly, send the agent what they ask for. If their website says 5,000 words and a covering letter, that is what you send them. Nothing else. If they ask for a synopsis and four chapters, again, that is what you must send. If they say don't submit unless you have a finished novel that they can ask for if they are interested, believe them and don't submit until you have finished your novel (as it happens, this should probably be your working assumption in any event).

That having been said, most agents will ask for three things: a **covering letter**, some **sample chapters** and a **synopsis**.

Let's look at them in turn.

THE COVERING LETTER

Writing is a profession and agents are particularly keen on authors who approach their craft in a business-like way. Authors who write often and to a high standard provide agents with regular novels to sell to publishers on their authors' behalf. Authors who conduct themselves professionally, both in their relationships with the agent but also everyone else they come into contact with in the publishing world, will always be preferred to those who do not. Your covering letter is a chance to show these things. With this in mind:

- **Spell the agent's name correctly.** It sounds pretty basic but if you're sending out ten letters, it's an easy mistake to make.
- **Be concise and to the point.** Agents are busy people. Tell them what they want to know and not much else.
- **Tell them why you are submitting to them in particular.** If an agent feels you have chosen them carefully that is (a) a sign that you are approaching this process in a business-like way and (b) a little bit flattering (agents are human beings too, mostly). If the agent represents an author that you believe you are very similar to, mention it. If you have met them at a festival or follow them on Twitter or have some other connection, mention that as well. If they have expressed an interest in a particular kind of novel, either in a blog post, or on their website, or wherever, mention it and explain why you think your novel is a match. You are trying to tell them that they are not just one of 100 submissions that you are sending out that day.
- **Briefly describe your novel.** You need to mention the title, the genre and the word count. You should also give a one paragraph description of the premise, why it is original and appealing. Sometimes it is helpful to compare it to other (ideally wildly successful) novels: 'It's *War and Peace* meets *One Flew Over the Cuckoo's Nest*', for example. You may be tempted to sell your novel – 'it's going to be next year's must-read' but you should probably resist puffing it up too much. At this stage, the agent only wants a taste of what is in store when they read the rest of your submission. However, if your novel is based on real persons, events or themes that will be of interest to a wide readership then these are a useful elements to highlight.

- **Tell them a little bit about yourself.** You don't need to go overboard – give a brief description of your background and obviously mention any interesting details that might make you stand out. If there is something distinct about you, or your connection to your novel, that might be a selling point for any possible publisher then you should mention it. For example, if you have written a novel about professional assassins that is based on your experiences as a police detective who specialised in tracking them down, then that would be a good thing to draw to an agent's attention. Similarly, if you have written a novel about a maritime disaster and you also happen to be a part-time volunteer with a lifeboat crew, then that is something you should let the agent know. Likewise, if you have had any writing successes such as winning a short story competition or have worked as writer in another format, such as film or journalism, then that will probably place your submission in a positive light.
- **Tell them why you wrote your novel.** What was it about the story that appealed to you in particular? Do you have a personal connection to the story? Although you should be honest, also think about what effect your reason will have on the agent. If you wrote a novel for a deeply personal reason, mention it if you feel comfortable doing so. If you have written the novel because you think it's a quick way to make easy money, probably keep that quiet.

If you don't have a personal connection or don't feel comfortable talking about yourself at this stage, that's fine. If your cover letter is professional and concise and tells the agent a little about the book it's probably done its job.

THE SYNOPSIS

Writing a good synopsis is probably the trickiest part of the submission process and it's a task that even professional writers with a number of novels under their belts struggle with. The good news is that the primary purpose of a synopsis is to give the agent an overview of the novel, reassuring them that it has a beginning, a middle and an end and a story that is clear, engaging and commercial. The quality of the synopsis itself is important, but not as important as you might think. If your novel has a good story and you follow a relatively straightforward format, then you should be able to produce a synopsis that will be adequate for its purpose. If your synopsis includes most of the following elements in an order that replicates the linear story of your novel, you should be just fine.

Start with a short, snappy summary of the story's concept

What you're trying to do here is hook the agent by giving them a sense of your novel's story and its setting, a flavour of its tone and a reason for them to look forward to the rest of the synopsis with some anticipation. The hook summary should only be a sentence or two long and placed in its own paragraph. You can differentiate the hook summary from the main body of the synopsis by placing it in italics and leaving a double line space between them. This is important as you may well repeat yourself between the two but the differentiation will make that acceptable. Finally, the hook summary is *not* essential and if it's proving too difficult or doesn't look quite right then you can always drop it altogether or wait until inspiration strikes. It is, however, a nice thing to have.

Let's look at an example. If we were writing a synopsis of *Pride and Prejudice,* we might start with a hook summary along the lines of the following.

> *In Georgian England, sparks fly when Miss Elizabeth Bennet, a proud young woman who believes she should only marry for love, meets the rich and aloof Mr Darcy. With misunderstandings aplenty, and circumstances separating them, will they be able to overcome their own pride and prejudice to find happiness together?*

Okay so it's a little tongue in cheek but it does give the agent important information about the story. Firstly, it identifies the main characters and tells the agent a little bit about them. It also explains that it's a love story and indicates when and where it's set. It outlines Elizabeth's objective, which is 'happiness together', along with some of the obstacles the characters will have to overcome before they achieve it. All in two sentences. Finally, the hook summary ends with a question that links into the title of the novel, which is an added bonus. Posing questions encourages the agent to read on.

See if you can do the same with your own novel.

Tell us who the central character is, what their situation is and why we like them. Indicate what their objective is over the course of the story.

Here we want to briefly introduce the central character, their situation, why we like them and what they are hoping to achieve. There will be some repetition from the hook summary (but that's okay).

> *Elizabeth Bennet is the second of five unmarried daughters to a rural gentleman of modest means. Her mother is concerned that her daughters should be wed to suitable husbands, but despairs of the intelligent and witty Elizabeth's desire to marry solely for love and mutual respect.*

This works to introduce Elizabeth by telling us that she is intelligent, witty and has admirable moral principles. It also reminds us of her objective (to marry for love) and tells us that her position is far from financially secure, which would have been a disadvantage at the time.

Tell us what event triggers the central character's engagement with the story. Introduce any other characters who will be particularly important to your story.

This is really the moment that Elizabeth's story begins, which in *Pride and Prejudice* is when she meets Mr Darcy.

> *When a desirable match, the amiable Bingley, rents a nearby estate, Elizabeth's older sister Jane is much taken with him. Bingley's friend, Darcy, is less appealing, seeming proud and conscious of his superior social and financial position, and Elizabeth and he clash. Darcy displays pride in his position and prejudice against those of lesser station and of less than perfect comportment (which biases him against Elizabeth and her family). Elizabeth displays pride in her own worth and prejudice against Darcy's perceived arrogance. And yet, there is a spark between them.*

Tell us about an initial obstacle that your central character must face and overcome, and establish their conflicts with other characters. Mention any characters who will help them.

Your novel will almost certainly contain obstacles and challenges. Generally, they will build in intensity, so try and replicate that incline in your synopsis.

> *Mr Collins, Elizabeth's unappealing cousin who will inherit her family home on her father's death, asks for her hand in marriage. She refuses, thinking that she could never love him. Her more pragmatic friend Charlotte accepts him, even though she doesn't love him, as the alternative is spinsterhood. Elizabeth's mother is furious but Jane and Mr Bennet are supportive.*

Clearly, if Elizabeth had accepted Collins, it would have been a short and very unsatisfactory novel but it still represents a bump in the road for Elizabeth. Fortunately, she sticks to her guns, even though this puts her into conflict with her mother, who wishes to see her married to someone of means, irrespective of their suitability. Jane and Mr Bennet's approval indicates that she has allies she can rely on.

Tell us about another obstacle, and mention any further conflicts that will help drive the story.

It is unlikely that your novel will have only one obstacle and they will probably come from conflict between Elizabeth and the other characters other than the ones you have already mentioned. You don't necessarily have to mention every conflict and obstacle but do mention the ones which are important to the story.

> *Sadly, Bingley soon departs, leaving Jane heartbroken, while the flirtatious Wickham, Darcy's estranged childhood companion, confirms Elizabeth's poor opinion of Darcy by telling her how Darcy deprived him of an inheritance. Elizabeth, visiting Charlotte and Mr Collins after Bingley's departure, encounters Darcy and discovers that he was responsible for separating Jane and Bingley.*

Elizabeth now has two good reasons not to like Darcy in addition to her earlier prejudiced view of him, so we are confirming that the conflict between them will be increased. Although we don't want to reveal it as yet, Wickham has misled Elizabeth and is not to be trusted.

Tell us about the inciting incident. The moment where the story takes a different direction.

The key plot points in your novel may not follow the exact structure that plotting experts may recommend, but there are going to be moments where the course of your story alters in a significant way. You need to mention them.

> *To her surprise, Darcy asks Elizabeth to marry him, which she refuses, confronting him about his behaviour to Jane and Wickham. The next day, Darcy delivers her a letter, revealing that Wickham lied about the inheritance, which Wickham did receive but gambled away. He also explains that Wickham attempted to seduce Darcy's fifteen-year-old sister as a means of securing his financial position. Elizabeth realises she may have been mistaken about Mr Darcy's character.*

Elizabeth is clearly surprised by Darcy's declaration, but she also realises that her forthright refusal was based on misunderstandings and misconceptions which, if her own pride and prejudices hadn't blinded her, she might have avoided.

Tell us about other significant steps that your central character takes to achieve their objective.

Your central character will occasionally be knocked back, or diverted, but they need to keep moving forward towards their objective. Mention the steps they are taking towards their goal.

> *Elizabeth returns to her family where her sisters continue to flirt with some militia officers, including Wickham. When Wickham and his brother officers are ordered to Brighton, Elizabeth's sister Lydia goes to stay with a friend who lives there, despite Elizabeth's reservations about her wont of good sense (and Wickham). Elizabeth, meanwhile, is invited on a sightseeing tour by her cousins the Gardiners. The trip includes a visit to Darcy's estate at Pemberley, where Elizabeth meets Darcy much to her embarrassment. However, he welcomes Elizabeth and the Gardiners wholeheartedly and Elizabeth regrets her earlier dismissal of him.*

All seems lost but Elizabeth, although certain that Darcy would not be present, allows herself to visit his very grand house. The encounter shows him to be kind and attentive and perhaps still well disposed to her. Maybe her initial reading of him as cold and arrogant was not entirely correct.

Tell us about a further obstacle your central character must overcome (the obstacles should continue to escalate).

It's often the case that the final obstacle places the central character in real danger. The danger may be physical but it may also be to their emotional wellbeing or to their position in society – but it must be significant.

> *A letter arrives with the news that Lydia has eloped with Wickham. Wickham is unlikely to marry Lydia, as she is penniless, but if Wickham does not marry her it will ruin her reputation and that of the entire family, including Elizabeth. After informing Darcy of their plight, Elizabeth and the Gardiners rush to find Wickham and Lydia before the elopement becomes known.*

In the novel, Darcy's reserve on hearing the news suggests that he has been confirmed in his earlier opinion of Elizabeth and her family and that all hope of a marriage is gone, but that is probably unnecessary for the synopsis.

Tell us about the central character's final challenge – when all seems lost.

Briefly indicate the steps your central character will take to overcome the challenge and how they contrive to be successful (or not).

> *Mr Bennet and Mr Gardiner search for the eloped couple to no avail. The sisters resign themselves to being unmarried and impoverished, but then Mr Gardiner sends news that the eloped couple have married after all. Mr Bennet rejoices and presumes that Mr Gardiner has paid off Wickham and wonders if he will ever be able to repay him. Instead it emerges that Darcy was their saviour. Elizabeth feels immense gratitude and realises just how wrong she was about Darcy.*

Elizabeth, as a woman in Georgian society, can't do much to overcome the challenge herself, so the actions that you would normally expect the central character to undertake are performed by her father, Mr Gardiner and Darcy. *Pride and Prejudice* is a novel of its time, when women were not entirely in control of their destiny. Although Elizabeth does her best to drive the story within the constraints of the period, she has limited flexibility. If you have a female character in a more egalitarian period, she should probably take much more control of the story.

Is there a further development before the final objective is achieved? How is the objective achieved? What happens next?

In order to know whether your novel is something that is publishable, the agent will need to know how it ends and it is essential that you are transparent about what happens in the synopsis. If you withhold the ending, perhaps hoping to intrigue them in some way, you run the risk of losing their interest instead. It is also a good idea to read back over your synopsis and if there are storylines that have not been completed, this is an opportunity to deal with them.

> *Bingley returns to his estate soon afterwards, with Darcy in tow, and duly proposes to Jane, who accepts. Darcy's intimidating aunt, with whom Elizabeth has had some previous run-ins, arrives unexpectedly and demands that Elizabeth tell her if Darcy has proposed. Elizabeth confirms he has not, which prompts the aunt to demand Elizabeth undertakes not to accept him should he do so. Elizabeth, standing up to her, refuses, wondering if this strange visit might mean that she can still have hope as regards Darcy. Sure enough, the next day Darcy asks for Elizabeth's hand in marriage.*

In my version of the synopsis, Darcy's aunt is not mentioned up to this moment because I have focussed on the most salient parts of the story. The aunt becomes significant at this point, as a final minor hurdle and an inadvertent sign of Elizabeth's possible happiness, so I need to mention her. I can address the earlier clashes between them as an aside. The key point is that Elizabeth has achieved her objective in marrying Darcy, a man she loves and admires, as he does her. In addition, the sub-plot between Jane and Bingley is addressed and by implication we know that the rest of Elizabeth's family are now content and financially secure.

Some final things to bear in mind.
I generally format my synopsis as four paragraphs. The first paragraph is my 'hook summary'. The second, third and fourth paragraphs relate to the beginning, middle and end of the novel. This allows me to show the plot of the novel clearly (my novels generally follow a three-act structure quite closely). The second paragraph, therefore, is where I introduce the main characters, the setting and the objective as well as mention any backstory that is important to the story. The third paragraph covers the middle of the novel and I expect this to take around half the total length of the synopsis, reflecting the proportion the middle act takes in the novel itself. This is where the escalating challenges, obstacles and conflicts go. The final paragraph covers the ending of the novel, where the goal is achieved after the final challenge is overcome. This is also where I tidy up any loose ends.

The synopsis should read smoothly and have a logical progression that mirrors the structure of the novel. The synopsis should focus on the story and should not include anything that does not either describe an event in the novel or explain why an event happens. So, in the example above, when Elizabeth rejects Collins, it is important the synopsis explains why, because it reflects her character's determination to stay true to her beliefs. Likewise, it is useful that the synopsis shows the changes in Elizabeth and Darcy's feelings for each other, as well as the chronological events.

I keep my first attempt at a synopsis to a maximum of 300 words, with a quarter for the beginning or set up, half for the middle and the remainder for the ending. I focus mainly on the key plot events in this draft, without much explanation as to why they happen. The next draft is 600 words, with the same proportional split as to word count; in this draft, I am trying to make sure it makes logical sense with the additions I make mainly being focussed on characterisation and explanation. My final draft will probably be around 1,000 words and the additions I make at this stage tend to be focussed on creating a smooth, entertaining and engaging read. The 300-word version is the most difficult to do but it does force me to identify the key plot points (because there really isn't much room for anything else).

An advantage of taking this three-stage approach is that you will have three different versions when submitting to agents, which may be useful as length requirements vary according to agency.

SAMPLE CHAPTERS

Your sample chapters, or extract, should generally be the beginning of your novel, as that is what most agencies ask for – and even if they don't, it's probably what they will be expecting. I have dealt with first chapters elsewhere, but there are some points that should probably be made again in the context of the submission process.

Your submission extract has to be as close to perfect as you can make it.
The first few chapters are the part of the novel that I always spend longest on. Although I've had five novels published at the time of writing, with two in the pipeline, I still have to give my editor an idea of how a new novel will read before she and the publisher will commit to it. In other words, I have to deliver them an extract that reflects the tone and style of the novel as well as, ideally, enthusing the editor and their colleagues that the novel I'm proposing is worth investing an advance in. The extract I deliver, much like the one you will probably deliver to an agent, will always be the first few chapters. I have a little bit of leeway because I've written several novels previously, but I still want those twenty or thirty pages to read very smoothly. I also want the extract to be devoid of any padding – everything has to be related to character, setting or story.

It has to sell your novel.
There are many different ways of starting a novel but it's worth remembering that you are submitting to an agent and you want to make them sit up and take notice and you probably have, at most,

three pages to get their attention. Remember how many submissions they get and remember how few of those submissions are successful. Remember also that many of those submissions will be written to a high standard and have good stories. Then ask yourself what is happening in those three pages to make your novel stand out from the others.

Excellent writing certainly helps but if there is nothing else but excellent writing, then it's probably not enough. The two pillars that a novel is built on are characters and story, so make sure something is happening in those first three pages that shows the agent that you can write good characters *and* tell a good story. If your novel begins with a lengthy description of a beautiful setting, consider whether you should perhaps start later – when the characters arrive and begin to interact and the story starts to move forward. There are lots of people who can write well but far fewer that can hold readers' attention with their storytelling.

Why do you need an agent and what do they do?

Let's presume that your synopsis, sample chapters and covering letter have attracted an agent's interest and they have decided they would like to represent you. The first thing you should do is meet them. This is an important relationship that you hope will last many years, ideally over a number of novels. Make sure, then, that you have similar expectations of the future and that you are confident they are the person you want to handle your career. Also check that you understand the contractual basis on which you will proceed. It is important that you have a contract in place that sets out the terms of your relationship as it will avoid any misunderstandings. Now that you are agented, you can also join The Society of Authors (www2.societyofauthors.org), an extremely useful organisation that has an advice service if you have any questions or doubts about the proposed contract.

Presuming that you and the agent are in agreement, their first task will be to introduce your novel to a wider world. As mentioned before, most UK publishers will not accept unsolicited manuscripts, so an agent is the key that unlocks access to them. An agent will also help you with your manuscript and represent your interests with your publishers. Agents are paid on a commission basis, so it is in their interests that your novel does as well as it possibly can and that your publishing career is long and successful. However, while they are very much on your side from a business point of view, they have also decided that they believe in you and your work. In other words, the relationship is not purely financial. They are often the shoulder you can cry on, the confidante you can express your concerns to and your biggest cheerleader when things go well. It is, in many ways, more of a partnership than anything else.

So what will your agent do for you?

They'll help you prepare your novel to submit to publishers

I know. Haven't we just been through the submission process? Surely, your agent just takes your submission and sends it straight out to the many eager publishers who await it? Well, if your novel really is perfect then that might be exactly what they will do. In most cases, however, some work will need to be done before it is ready to be sent out. Even if you have had a freelance editor and a creative writing teacher or mentor helping you with your manuscript, they will not have been looking at it in the same way as an agent will. Your novel is now a 'product' that your agent will sell on your behalf. Agents are paid a percentage of any advances, royalties or other earnings that your novel and any future novels receive. We'll talk more about the types of earnings your novel may attract below but the point to make here is that the agent earns money for your novel *based on its success*. When they take you on, in other words, they are attracted by the potential of you and your novel as a business proposition. Their motivation is not solely commercial, of course, but a large part of it is, and should be.

So, what is your agent going to do to improve the likelihood of you and your novel being successful? First, they are going to almost certainly want you to rewrite it based, at least to make in part, on their wanting to make it as attractive to publishers (and readers) as they can. Nearly always, this means they want to make your novel better – so it's a good thing. Sometimes, however, an agent will want changes to your novel that you don't feel comfortable with. As it will be your name on the cover, not the agent's, if you don't want to make the changes they suggest, and they don't think they can sell your novel without those changes, then it may be best if you find a different agent to represent you. The good news is that this seldom happens – good agents know a lot about novels and are very skilled at this part of the process.

They'll try to find you a publisher

Each fiction publishing house is a little bit like a factory and, to remain in business, they need to regularly publish new books. Each publishing house therefore retains a stable of authors contracted to produce this steady flow of titles and managed by the editors that work for it with successful authors signing book deals for multiple new novels, scheduled for several years in advance. Each editor within a publishing house has a separate list that they publish, often with different requirements. Some editors will only publish, for example, crime fiction and others will publish a much wider list with a range of very different genres. The authors that write for an editor's list move on regularly, so editors are always on the lookout for promising new authors. To meet this need for new authors, there is a constant conversation between agents and editors, with editors informing agents of the kinds of authors they are looking for.

Once you have redrafted your novel to the point where both you and your agent are happy for it to be introduced to the publishing world, your agent will get to work on the sales part of their job. In reality, they will probably have been talking to potential editors about your novel from the moment they took you on, especially if they know that a particular editor is looking for a novel which is similar to yours. Your agent will begin the sales process by identifying the strengths of the novel and deciding how they will present it. If your novel has resemblances, even quite remote, to recently published novels that have done very well, your agent will probably make use of those comparisons. Likewise, some novels can fall into different categories so how the novel is presented to a particular editor may also shape how it is received. Your agent will tailor a cover letter to present your novel in the most favourable light to each editor. Ideally your agent is hoping for more than one editor to be interested, and they will also be considering how to sell other rights, such as for film and television and translation. With this in mind, they may hold off on submitting to editors until one of the big book fairs, such as London or Frankfurt (particularly if they think you have a very commercial novel).

Your agent is trying to do two things here: first, create anticipation and competition between different UK publishing houses; and second, create a buzz around your novel which they hope will be picked up by the publishing-focussed media – *The Bookseller* and *Publishers Weekly*, for example. If they can interest two or more UK editors to the point that they will bid against each other for the right to publish your novel (and perhaps some further novels as well), chances are you'll be paid more money for your novel than if only one editor bids. If your agent has done their job very well, and your novel is very good, then an editor may attempt a pre-emptive offer. This will be designed to be generous enough for you to accept without waiting for counter offers.

The advantage of your novel being pre-empted or the subject of a bidding war is that word of your novel's success will spread. If your agent has delayed submitting until just before a book fair, and they have retained world rights, then you may well have publishers from other countries keen to consider translating your novel. Your agency may have dedicated translation and film and television agents who will work on your behalf with regard to these rights.

Throughout this process, your agent will be trying to find an editor who they think will be most suitable for your novel and your career. Some editors are better than others when it comes to nurturing new authors, with some editors and publishing houses excelling at publishing debut novels successfully, while not perhaps paying the largest advances. Sometimes, when there are two offers on the table, your agent will suggest that you take the one that pays less initially. If they're doing that, it's probably because they believe that your interests (and theirs) are better served by taking a longer-term view of the choices on offer. Which brings us to the next stage of the process.

Negotiating a book deal

Your agent will have considerable experience of dealing with the nuts and bolts of how your contract will work with the publisher. Here are some of the things they will take into account:

- **The size of the advance.** An advance is the payment made by the publisher to the writer against anticipated future sales of a novel. If you fulfil your contractual commitments, in terms of delivering novels of publishable quality to the publisher on the dates that you are required to do so, then the advance is not repayable.

  When publishers look at established authors, they take into account the potential of the novel and the sales track record of the novelist's previous titles. This can mean that excellent novels attract very small advances. With debut novelists, the publishers have no track record to look at, so they are largely guessing as to how they think it will sell based on its quality and originality. This can result in advances that are too large (and, possibly more often, too small). The disadvantage with very large advances is that a publisher often struggles to achieve sufficient revenue from sales to cover them. Indeed, if sales are disappointing, the contract will represent a loss to the publisher which they will take account of when negotiating any future deals. In most professions, the initial remuneration represents a base point, from which there is an upward trajectory This is, unfortunately, not always the case in publishing. It is sometimes, from a long-term point of view, better to start with a reasonable advance that you are more likely to earn out from sales of the contacted novels.

- **When the money is paid and in what proportions.** You don't get the advance all at once. Generally, it is paid in quarters or thirds, with thirds being paid on: (a) signature of the contract; (b) acceptance by the publisher of a manuscript that you deliver; and (c) first publication of the novel. If your novel is published in both hardback and paperback, a final quarter may be payable on paperback publication. Although most advances are divided into equal payments, your agent may try and get a larger proportion of the advance paid earlier.
- **What publishing rights are covered.** The UK publisher will generally license either UK and Commonwealth rights (which will give the publisher the right to publish in English-speaking countries other than the US) or world rights, in which case the publisher licences all publishing rights, often selling them on to foreign publishers, with the revenue from those sales going towards your advance. They will almost certainly purchase both digital and print rights. Other rights which the

publisher may want to have covered by the contract are audio rights and film, television and other dramatic performance rights.

- **Number of novels to be delivered (and when).** You may be very happy to have your novel published, but your agent will be hoping that you will publish further novels on a regular basis. They will try to persuade your publisher to commit to more than one novel, along with reasonable delivery dates.

There will be other details as well, sometimes related to publicity and marketing commitments. If you have any doubts about the contract that is negotiated and you are a member of The Society of Authors then, as mentioned before, they have a contract advice service which can provide very useful objective guidance.

Managing your relationship with your publishers

As a debut novelist, you probably won't have too much idea of how the publishing world works. You should, however, be able to rely on your agent to guide you. It is in their interests, after all, that the publisher publishes your novel successfully.

As soon as the contract is signed, and sometimes even beforehand, your editor will start editing your novel. The first edit that they will do will be the 'structural edit' where they focus on the story and make certain that your novel has a beginning, a middle and an end and that the most is made of the story and the characters. They will make suggestions for changes, which may be substantial, and will expect you rewrite the novel taking account of these edits. Your agent will be there to tell you not to worry, that the editor still loves your novel, but they want to make it even better. You may have been through five or six edits already at this stage and there may be some changes that you feel will change the story beyond recognition.

If there is a sticking point, your agent will work, on your behalf, to get past it.

After the structural edit is finished (and there may be two or maybe even three rewrites before that happens), the editor will do a 'line edit'. This will be more focussed on language, prose and minor details. The good news is that you are now on the home stretch and your novel is very close to being published, but there will still be problems that need fixing. This may also be the time when you start to discuss the title. You may have a preferred title in mind, but the sales and editorial teams will be looking to aim the novel at the widest possible audience. Personally, I am happy to go with the title the publisher suggests. I do however, care very much about covers and this may also be the stage where you, and your agent, will be shown sample covers. If you are unhappy with the covers you are shown, let your agent do the negotiation. It's what they are paid to do and they will be able to be much more aggressive (and objective) than you will.

The line edits completed, you will now be introduced to the 'copy-edit', where a specialist copy-editor, generally freelance, will go over your novel looking for tiny mistakes and inaccuracies as well as ensuring a consistency of style. They will probably find a great deal more than you would have expected because after a certain point of rewriting it's not unusual to lose track of details.

Once the copy-edit is completed, the novel will be formatted for printing and you will be presented with the page proofs. This is not the time to decide that you would like to rewrite an entire chapter. The novel is finished now and all you should be looking for are spelling mistakes and other minor errors. It's also when you get to see what the book will look like when it is printed, so it's exciting.

At this stage, in the run up to publication day, your agent will probably get more involved. They will want to know what the publicity and marketing campaigns are going to be for the novel. They will also be answering your many questions about the publishing process and supporting you when you need it. The more work the publisher does on publicity and marketing, the higher the chance that the sales team within the publisher will have success selling the books into bookshops. Your agent will be fighting your corner, ensuring that your novel gets as much support as possible from the publisher.

What do agents charge?

Needless to say, for all of the work that they will do on your behalf, the agent will need to be paid. Your agent will generally charge you 15 per cent (plus VAT) of any revenue you receive from a UK publisher as a result of their efforts – so it is in your agent's interest that your novel is as successful as possible.

Unless a UK publisher licenses the world rights to your novel, your agent will also be responsible for selling the translation rights to your novel on a country by country basis. The bigger UK agencies will have dedicated translation agents within the agency who will liaise with foreign publishers and sub-agents. Because the selling of translation rights is more complex and often relies on the use of local sub-agents, the agent will generally receive 20 per cent (plus VAT) of any revenue. If your publisher has purchased world rights, they will sell the foreign rights on your behalf, often also charging 20 per cent (plus VAT), and offsetting any revenue against the advance you have received.

The best way to explain how translation rights work differently when a publisher rather than an agent looks after them is to look at an example. Let's say your novel attracts a £20,000 advance from a UK publisher and three foreign advances of £10,000 each.

If the UK publisher has licensed UK and Commonwealth rights, you will receive £16,400 for the UK rights, (£20,000 less the agent's fee (at 15 per cent) of £3000 + £600 VAT). In respect of the foreign deals, you will receive £22,800 (£30,000 less the combined agent's fees of £6000 (at 20 per cent) + £1,200 VAT). You will therefore receive £39,200 in total.

If, on the other hand, your agent has sold world rights to the UK publisher, they will charge the same fees and also pay off the £20,000 advance you received before you get to see any of the revenue from the foreign deals. In this scenario, you will receive £22,800, less your £20,000 original advance, leaving you with £2,800. Your agent will pass that on, also taking their fees of £420 + VAT of £84, leaving you with £2,296 for the foreign rights.

As opposed to the £39,200 you receive under UK rights and foreign rights being handled by your agent, you will receive £18,696 for the world rights handled by your publisher.

It's not as bad as it looks, however. You have now earned out your advance, which is an achievement for a debut novelist. The other good news is that any future foreign advances for this novel will be paid to you in full (less, of course, the fees charged by both the publisher and the agent) as well as any royalties in UK sales. If your UK publisher has paid you a very large advance for world rights, you may not mind too much; if there is only a small world rights advance on offer, though, it is as well to be aware of the fact that you will be double-charged fees on any translation deals.

It is also worth bearing in mind that translation advances are also paid in instalments, just as with UK advances, with equal proportions being paid on signature, delivery of the script and acceptance, first publication and paperback publication (if relevant). If you have sold world rights to your UK publisher, under the preceding example, you would be unlikely to receive any payment until some considerable time after the translation agreements are signed.

Finally, your agent, or a partner agency, will attempt to sell film, television and radio rights to your novel. Their fees for this are a standard 15 per cent + VAT.

Summary

SUBMITTING TO AN AGENT

- Research literary agents and identify those who you think would be a good fit for you and your novel. Draw up a short-list of the top ten agents you wish to submit to.
- Familiarise yourself with your chosen agent/s current list of authors, what they do and do not represent, and their submission guidelines. All will be available on their agency's website.
  - Do not engage with an agent who charges a 'reading fee'. No money should be exchanged before the agent has agreed to represent you and the necessary contracts signed.
- Send out submissions adhering to the agent's specific guidelines. This will usually consist of a covering letter, sample chapters and synopsis.
- Send out a few submissions at a time and make note of the response times given by the agents, which can be up to three months.
  - They may request the full MS. They may still reject it, but this is a positive start.
- Many great writers have received rejection letters. Do not be disheartened when an agent says 'No'.
  - If you receive a personalised rejection, take note of any feedback they give you and consider revising your MS based on this.

Do	Don't
The covering letter	

• **Do** personalise every submission.
• **Do** spell the agent's name correctly and use their preferred pronouns.
• **Do** follow the submission guidelines.
• **Do** write a concise covering letter:
  ○ **Do** include the title, genre and word count.
  ○ **Do** describe your novel in one paragraph.
  ○ **Do** include comparison titles.
  ○ **Do** include why you are submitting to them specifically.
  ○ **Do** write a brief note about yourself.
	• **Do not** submit unless you have a full manuscript.
	• **Do not** send out a blanket submission or generic covering letter.
	• **Do not** include any extras in your submission that are not specified, e.g. cover illustration.
	• **Do not** submit under a pen name.

The synopsis	
• **Do** keep your synopsis to one page. • **Do** give an overview of the book's story arc. • **Do** include key plot points.	• **Do not** hide the ending or twist from the agent. • **Do not** include every single event. • **Do not** list every character in the book.
The sample chapters	
• **Do** include the opening chapters (usually the first three). • **Do** format the chapters to requested standard (usually double-spaced, 12pt Times New Roman, number pages). • **Do** include your name and contact details in the document.	• **Do not** send unless you are sure the opening chapters are perfect. • **Do not** include a selection of chapters. • **Do not** use unprofessional fonts, layouts or include illustrations.

Submission Dos and Don'ts

Resources

Example synopsis

In Georgian England, sparks fly when Miss Elizabeth Bennet, a proud young woman who believes she should only marry for love, meets the rich and aloof Mr Darcy. With misunderstandings aplenty, and circumstances separating them, will they be able to overcome their own pride and prejudice to find happiness together?

Elizabeth Bennet is the second of five unmarried daughters to a rural gentleman of modest means. Her mother is concerned that her daughters should be wed to suitable husbands, but despairs of the intelligent and witty Elizabeth's desire to marry solely for love and mutual respect.

When a desirable match, the amiable Bingley, rents a nearby estate, Elizabeth's older sister Jane is much taken with him. Bingley's friend, Darcy, is less appealing, seeming proud and conscious of his superior social and financial position, and Elizabeth and he clash. Darcy displays pride in his position and prejudice against those of lesser station and of less than perfect comportment (which biases him against Elizabeth and her family). Elizabeth displays pride in her own worth and prejudice against Darcy's perceived arrogance. And yet, there is a spark between them.

Mr Collins, Elizabeth's unappealing cousin who will inherit her family home on her father's death, asks for her hand in marriage. She refuses, thinking that she could never love him. Her more pragmatic friend Charlotte accepts him, even though she doesn't love him, as the alternative is spinsterhood. Elizabeth's mother is furious but Jane and Mr Bennet are supportive.

Sadly, Bingley soon departs, leaving Jane heartbroken, while the flirtatious Wickham, Darcy's estranged childhood companion, confirms Elizabeth's poor opinion of Darcy by telling her how Darcy deprived him of an inheritance. Elizabeth, visiting Charlotte and Mr Collins after Bingley's departure, encounters Darcy and discovers that he was responsible for separating Jane and Bingley. To her surprise, Darcy asks Elizabeth to marry him, which she refuses, confronting him about his behaviour to Jane and Wickham. The next day, Darcy delivers her a letter, revealing that Wickham lied about the inheritance, which Wickham did receive but gambled away. He also explains that Wickham attempted to seduce Darcy's fifteen-year-old sister as a means of securing his financial position. Elizabeth realises she may have been mistaken about Mr Darcy's character.

Elizabeth returns to her family where her sisters continue to flirt with some militia officers, including Wickham. When Wickham and his brother officers are ordered to Brighton Elizabeth's sister Lydia goes to stay with a friend who lives there, despite Elizabeth's reservations about her wont of good sense (and Wickham). Elizabeth, meanwhile, is invited on a sightseeing tour by her cousins the Gardiners. The trip includes a visit to Darcy's estate at Pemberley, where Elizabeth meets Darcy much to her embarrassment. However, he welcomes Elizabeth and the Gardiners wholeheartedly and Elizabeth regrets her earlier dismissal of him.

A letter arrives with the news that Lydia has eloped with Wickham. Wickham is unlikely to marry Lydia, as she is penniless, and if Wickham does not marry Lydia it will ruin her reputation and that of the entire family, including Elizabeth. After informing Darcy of their plight, Elizabeth and the Gardiners rush to find Wickham and Lydia before the elopement becomes known. Mr Bennet and Mr Gardiner search for the eloped couple to no avail. All seems lost and the sisters resign themselves to being unmarried and impoverished, but then Mr Gardiner sends news that the eloped couple have married after all. Mr Bennet rejoices and presumes that Mr Gardiner has paid off Wickham. Instead it emerges that Darcy was their saviour. Elizabeth feels immense gratitude and realises just how wrong she was about Darcy.

Bingley returns to his estate soon afterwards, with Darcy in tow, and duly proposes to Jane, who accepts. Darcy's intimidating aunt, with whom Elizabeth has had some previous run-ins, arrives unexpectedly and demands that Elizabeth tell her if Darcy has proposed. Elizabeth confirms he has not, which prompts the aunt to demand Elizabeth undertakes not to accept him should he do so. Elizabeth, standing up to her, refuses, wondering if this strange visit might mean that she can still have hope as regards Darcy. Sure enough, the next day Darcy asks for her hand in marriage.

Software for writers

Many software packages and apps are available to writers to aid them with writing, productivity, project management and editing. I have mentioned a few products I personally use in this *Guide*, but the market is awash with different options to suit your individual writing style, budget and requirements.

Below is a selection of readily available and popular software that may prove useful to you on your novel writing journey. I recommend you research the products thoroughly, especially the cost and whether the software will be compatible with your other writing equipment. What works for one writer may not work for you, so make use of the free trials many of the developers offer and find what suits you best.

Writing software

Aeon Timeline

www.aeontimeline.com
£42 one-off fee

Includes tools and features to help you understand characters, avoid plot holes and inconsistencies, and visualise your story in new ways.

Bibisco

https://bibisco.com
Community edition – Free; Supporters' edition – pay what you want

Designed to allow a writer to focus on their characters and develop rounded and complex narratives, with particular emphasis on the manuscript's geographical, temporal and social context.

Dabble

www.dabblewriter.com
from $48 p.a.

Gives writers the freedom to plot, write and edit on a desktop, in a browser or offline, and automatically syncs all versions across your devices. Features include plot grids, progress-tracking and goal-setting.

FocusWriter
https://gottcode.org/focuswriter
Free

Provides a simple and distraction-free writing environment with a hide-away interface, so you can focus solely on your writing.

FreeWriter
www.freewritersoftware.com
Free

Contains all the functionality you need to format and organise documents, including spell-checking, full dictionary, extensive thesaurus, global search and replace, automatic voice read-back and also speech recognition. There are facilities to help you build robust story elements, so that you can profile characters, places, ideas and plot themes, each within their own module. Helpfully, there are also tools to enable you to set productivity targets, and plot your progress against these.

Novelize
www.getnovelize.com
$65 p.a.

Developed for fiction writers, this web-based writing app means you can work on your book anywhere on any device. Keep your research in one place in the notebook displayed on the writing screen and track your progress.

Novel Factory
www.novel-software.com
from $75 p.a.

Plan your book with confidence by using the Roadmap feature which provides tools and structures to suit your needs. Includes detailed character overviews including biographies and images, as well as scene tabs and writing statistics about your work.

Novel Suite
www.novelsuite.com/novel-writing-software
$99 p.a.

An all-in-one novel writing application that can be used across all devices. Manage multiple books using character profiles, scene outlines and writing template tools.

Scrivener
www.literatureandlatte.com/scrivener/overview
£47 one-off fee

One-stop solution tailored for long writing projects: it is a typewriter, ring binder and scrapbook all at once, which allows you to optimise your digital workspace.

SmartEdit Writer
www.smart-edit.com/Writer
Free

Helps you to build your book organically one scene or one chapter at a time, then drag and drop to arrange these on your document tree. You can also store your research images, URLs and notes alongside work for easy access, and export your manuscript into a single Word document when ready.

Ulysses
https://ulysses.app
£48.99 p.a.

Document management for all writing projects, with flexible export options including pdf, Word, ebook and HTML, which are appropriately formatted and styled.

Wavemaker

https://wavemaker.co.uk/
Free

Open-source app designed to sync easily across all your devices. Includes a range of different planning tools to suit your writing style (e.g. cards, timeline and grid). Work offline for distraction-free writing, make notes, store notes, photos and research in a taggable, searchable database.

WriteItNow

www.ravensheadservices.com
$59.95 one-off fee

Includes sophisticated world-building features to create detailed and complex settings and characters. Recommends suitable names for your characters based on the historical period and geographical setting of your story.

Editing software

After the Deadline

www.afterthedeadline.com
Free

A context-driven grammar and spelling checker that underlines potential issues and gives a suggestion with an explanation of how you can rectify errors.

AutoCrit
www.autocrit.com
Free

Analyses your entire manuscript and suggests insightful improvements in the form of an individual summary report, showing where your strengths and weaknesses lie.

Grammarly
www.grammarly.com
Free

Provides accurate and context-specific suggestions when the application detects grammar, spelling, punctuation, word choice and style mistakes in your writing.

Hemingway Editor
www.hemingwayapp.com
$19.99 one-off fee

Helps you write with clarity and confidence. This application is like a spellchecker, but for style. It will highlight any areas that need tightening up by identifying: adverbs, passive voice, and uninspiring or over-complicated words.

ProWritingAid
https://prowritingaid.com
£79 p.a.

For use via the web, or as an add-on to word processing software, it interrogates your work for a multitude of potential issues such as passive voice, clichés, missing dialogue tags and pace, and suggests how you can rectify any errors or make style improvements.

SmartEdit

www.smart-edit.com
$77 one-off fee

Sits inside Microsoft Word and runs twenty-five individual checks while you work, flagging areas that need attention, including: highlighting repeated words, listing adverbs and foreign phrases used and identifying possible misused words.

WordRake

www.wordrake.com
$129 p.a.

When you click the 'rake' button in Microsoft Word, the text editor will read your document and suggest edits to tighten and add clarity to your work.

Index

accent of character 68, 106, 182–3
acknowledgements 49
action 20, 34, 165, 186
act one: the beginning 119–26
  aims and motivations 123
  central character engagement with story 124–6
  characters and personalities 120–1
  dramatic world 122–3
  first chapters and prologues 116
  length of 126
  objectives 124
  overview 119, 140
  sample chapters 209–10
  three-act structure 115
act two: the middle 126–36
  conflict 127–8
  driving the story 134–5
  internal issues 129
  midpoint event 132–3
  objectives 127
  overview 126–7, 141
  pace 133–4
  risk 134
  series of obstacles and challenges 130–2
  significant event and final ordeal 135–6
  sources of obstacles and challenges 129–30
  three-act structure 115
act three: the end 136–40
  final challenge 136–7
  final twist or surprise 137–8
  overview 136, 142
  pleasing conclusion 138–9
  sub-plots 139
  three-act structure and alternatives 115, 139–40
adjectives 32
advances 214–15, 218, 219
adverbs 32, 185
agencies 195, 196, 218
agents
  charges and costs 218–19
  checking the novel is finished 191
  covering letter 198–200
  finding a publisher 212–14
  identifying an agent 193–8
  managing relationship with publishers 216–17
  negotiating a book deal 214–16
  preparing the novel for submission 211–12
  sample chapters 209–10
  submissions overview 220–1
  submitting to an agent 198–210
  synopsis 200–9
  why you need an agent and what they do 210–14
age of character 65–6
all-seeing (omniscient) narration 18, 21, 24–5, 35
animal life 51, 52
antipathies 101, 102, 162
appearance *see* physical appearance of character

apps 4, 7–8
atmosphere 39, 40, 118, 119, 145, 146, 147
attraction between characters 100–1, 162
attractiveness of character 67, 82, 101
audio rights 216
authenticity 37, 38, 45, 48

background noise 4
backstory 70–1, 76, 105
backups 7
Baedeker travel guides 41
basics 15–35
- adverbs and adjectives 32
- conveying information 34
- descriptions 29–31
- first-person POV, third-person POV or omniscient 21–5
- general points 29–34
- important moments 32–3
- logic and credibility 33–4
- overview 15, 35
- point of view (POV) 18–19
- point of view guidelines 25–7
- single POV or multiple POVs 19–21
- tenses 27–9
- why this novel 15–18
- words and sentences 31–2

beginning of novel *see* act one: the beginning
bidding wars 213, 214
blockers 4
blogs 195, 199
book covers 217
book deals 214–16
book fairs 213, 214
The Bookseller 194, 213
bookshops 218
book titles 217

carrying dialogue 184–8
central characters 61–87
- age 65–6
- backstory 70–1
- body shape 67
- building a central character 63–81
- capacity to change 81
- capacity to surprise 80–1
- carrying the novel 84–5
- choosing the right central character 86
- conflict 77, 102–4, 127–8, 157
- current situation 71–2
- dress 68
- driving the story 62, 134–5
- ending a scene 165–6
- enemies 74
- engagement with story 124–6
- extraordinary abilities 80
- first chapters and prologues 117–18
- first impressions 64–5
- friends and loved ones 73–4
- gender and sex 66
- health 68–9
- height 66–7
- internal issues 77, 129
- living arrangements 75
- motivation 78–9
- name 70
- objectives 124, 127, 148
- obstacles and challenges 129–32, 136–7
- omniscient narration 24
- overview 61–3, 87
- pastimes and interests 75–6
- personality 76–81

physical appearance 64–5, 67–9, 82–3
physical attractiveness 67
pleasing conclusion 138–9
point of view 18, 19–21, 22, 23–4
profession 72–3
race and ethnicity 69
reader engagement 63
revealing the central character 81–4
risk 134
speech 68
state of mind 73
and subsidiary characters 75, 89, 90–3, 98, 102–4
synopsis 202
telling the scene 152, 154, 155
telling the story 62–3
virtues 77–8
chairs 3, 10
challenges
final challenge 136–7
research 46
scenes 148–9, 157
series of obstacles and challenges 130–2
sources of obstacles and challenges 129–30
change, capacity to 81
chapters
first chapters and prologues 115–19
important moments 32
numbering 5
sample chapters 209–10
and scenes 143–5
characters
attraction between 100–1, 162
central characters 61–87
conflict between 127–8
conveying information 34
dialogue 169–70, 182–3
dramatic world 110, 111
interaction between 75, 183–4
logic and credibility 33
managing characters 104–6
objectives 124, 127, 148
point of view 18–19, 22–6
research 39, 43, 44
sample chapters 210
subsidiary characters 89–107
who is telling the scene 151–5
see also central characters; subsidiary characters
charges and costs 218–19
children's fiction 194
class 106
cliché 187
climate 52
clothing 65, 68
cloud backups 7
codes of behaviour 112–13
Commonwealth *see* UK and Commonwealth rights
completion date 2
compromise 180–4
computers 3, 5, 7
conclusion of novel 138–9; *see also* act three: the end
confidentiality 49
conflict
central character 62, 72, 73, 77, 79, 84, 102–4
conflict, risk, obstacles and subtext 156–62
dialogue and motivation 177, 179
driving the story 62
omniscient narration 24
plot 111, 123, 127–8
researching context 43, 46
scenes 156, 157–8, 162

subsidiary characters 91–2, 102–4
synopsis 204
consistency 104, 217
contemporary fiction 18, 38, 49, 118
context 42–8, 58
contracts 210–11, 215, 216
control
dialogue 173–7
scenes 162–4
controversial issues 43
conversations *see* dialogue
conveying information 30, 34, 147–8
copy-editing 217
costs and charges 218–19
courses, writing 10, 211
covering letters 198–200, 213, 221
cover of book 217
Covid pandemic 44
crafts 51
Creative England 10
Creative Scotland 10
creative writing courses 10, 211
credibility 33–4, 56, 100, 184
crime writing
central character 70, 78, 85
choosing a theme 16
finished novel and agents 196, 212
first-person POV 22
plot 110, 112, 113, 132, 137, 140–2
research 49, 55
subsidiary characters 89, 90, 97, 99
crisis, final 149
cuts files 6

danger 92, 158–9, 166
deadlines and target dates 2, 8, 11
deals 214–16
debut novelists 196, 214, 215, 216, 219
descriptions 20, 29–31, 105, 186
desks 2, 10
detective novels 16–17, 55, 70, 89–90, 113, 180
dialogue 169–89
carrying dialogue 184–8
compromise 180–4
control 173–7
dialogue-carrying verbs 184–5
managing characters 105–6
motivation 170–1, 177–80
overview 188–9
point of view 20, 23
purpose of 169–73
revealing the central character 83
scene telling 155
dictation 3, 8
digital rights 215
disability 68–9
dislikes 101, 170
distractions 4, 11
drafts 3, 5, 6, 208
dramatic world 109, 110–14, 122–3, 146–7
driving the story 62, 134–5
dystopian fiction 119

earnings
advances 214–15, 218, 219
royalties 211, 219
ear plugs 4
editing
copy-editing 217
line editing 193, 216–17
software 231–3
structural editing 216–17

editors 193, 195–7, 211, 212–13, 214, 216–17
email 4, 7
emotion 16–17, 182, 187
endings
 false endings 132
 plot 138–9
 scenes 164–6
 sub-plots 139
 synopsis 207
 see also act three: the end
enemies, of character 74, 101
equipment, researching 48, 50–1
errors 25, 50, 217
ethnicity 69, 103
events
 midpoint event 131–2
 real events 56
 significant events 135–6, 172
exercise, for health 10–11
extracts 209–10

false endings 132
family 101, 111–12, 113
fantasy fiction 38, 118, 196
feedback 9, 192–3, 197
festivals 194, 199
film rights 213, 214, 216, 219
final challenge 136–7, 149, 205–7
final draft 6, 208
final twist 137–8
finances *see* money matters
finished novel 191–221
 checking it is finished 191–3
 covering letter 198–200
 identifying an agent 193–8
 managing relationship with publishers 216–18
 negotiating a book deal 214–16
 overview 191, 220–1
 sample chapters 209–10
 submitting to an agent 198–210
 synopsis 200–9
 what agents charge 218–19
 why you need an agent and what they do 210–14
firearms research 50
first act *see* act one: the beginning
first chapters 115–19, 209–10
first drafts 3, 5
first impressions of character 64–5
first-person POV (point of view) 21–3, 24, 35
five W's (where, when, who, what, why) 167
flaws of character 77, 129
foreign publishers 215, 218
foreign rights 218–19
formatting 5, 208
Frankfurt Book Fair 213
freelance copy-editors 217
freelance editors 193, 211
friends and loved ones of character 73–4, 101
frontal adverbials 31–2
future novels 216

gender and sex 43–5, 63, 66, 206–7
genre 85, 196
genre fiction 97
getting started 1–13
 cuts files 6
 formatting 5
 minimising distractions 4
 notebooks and story ideas 8
 overview 11–13
 place to write 2–3
 protecting work 7

quantity and quality 5
rewriting 5–6
staying healthy 10–11
targets and progress 2
technology and software 7–8
time management 1
what to write with 3–4
writers' groups 9
writing courses 10
ghost stories 20, 85, 119
Google Streetview 42
grammar 8, 192
groups of characters 61–2, 114, 134
guns research 50

handling research 53–6, 59
handwriting 3, 7, 8
hardback publication 215
headphones 4
health 10–11, 67, 68–9
hidden elements 94, 97–8, 121, 160, 181
historians 51
historical fiction 16, 40, 44–6
home
character's living arrangements 75
distractions 4
place to write 2–3
hooks 119, 165, 166
hook summary 201–2, 208
horror fiction 20
humour 19, 72, 73, 75, 84, 150

identifying an agent 193–8
images 46–8, 52
inciting incident 125, 140, 204
independent publishers 194
information, conveying 30, 34, 147–8
inside knowledge 48–51
Instagram 195
interaction between characters 75, 183–4
internal issues of character 77, 129
internal monologue 165
internet 4, 42
internet forums 49, 50
interviews 52
Irish Writers Centre 10

jargon 183
journalism 200

keyboards 10

language, in dialogue 182–3
laptops 3, 4, 7, 8, 10
letters
covering letters 198–200, 213, 221
in research 48
libel 56
libraries 3, 41, 52
line editing 193, 216–17
literary agents *see* agents
Literature Wales 10
living arrangements of character 75
living subjects 56
location 38–42, 52, 84, 146
logic 33–4, 99–100
London Book Fair 213
longhand writing 3, 7, 8
loose ends 25, 35, 136, 146, 149, 208
losing work 7

maps 41
marketing 216, 217–18
media 213
medieval locations 41

memoirs 53
memories 39
memory sticks 7
mentors 211
middle of novel *see* act two: the middle
midpoint event 131–2
mirrors, character use of 20, 65, 82
misdirection 98, 172, 179
misunderstandings 44, 68, 98–9, 172, 181, 210
mixing tenses and POVs 29
mobile phones 3, 4, 7, 8, 51
money matters
- advances 214–15, 218, 219
- agents' charges 218–19
- finding a publisher 213
- royalties 211, 219

motivation
- central character 70, 78–9, 86, 102–3
- dialogue 170–1, 177–80
- plot aims and motivations 123
- scenes and conflict 158
- subsidiary characters 90, 94, 95–6, 97, 102–3

movement 186
multiple POVs (points of view) 19–21, 26–7, 35, 62–3, 152
murder mysteries 90, 110–11, 113, 157–8, 160, 162–3, 165
museums 48, 51, 52
music 4

name of character 70
narration
- dialogue 186–7
- omniscient narration 18, 21, 24–5, 35
- point of view guidelines 25–7
- *see also* point of view

narrative purpose of scene 164
nationality of character 182–3
natural world 51–2
negotiating a book deal 214–16
newspapers 48
noise-reduction headphones 4
non-fiction 24
notebooks 7, 8
notes 7, 8, 40, 52, 53
novel writing
- the basics 15–35
- central characters 61–87
- dialogue 169–89
- finished novel 191–221
- getting started 1–13
- plot 109–42
- research, atmosphere and setting 37–59
- resources 225–33
- subsidiary characters 89–107
- why this novel 15–18
- writing scenes 143–67

objectives
- central characters 78, 82, 124, 127, 148
- and motivation 78, 95–6
- plot 124, 127
- scenes 148, 157
- subsidiary characters 90–2, 95–8, 102–4
- synopsis 205, 207

observation 34, 165
obstacles
- central character 62, 69, 74, 104
- conflict, risk, obstacles and subtext 156–62
- plot 129–32
- researching context 46
- scenes 148–9, 156, 157, 159–60

series of obstacles and challenges 130–2
sources of obstacles and challenges 129–30
subsidiary characters 92, 104
synopsis 203, 204, 205
offers 213–14
omniscient (all-seeing) narration 18, 21, 24–5, 35
opening chapters 82, 115–19
opening scene 122
Open University 10
organising your time 1
over-writing 119

pace 28, 133–4
'page 64' problem 127
page proofs 217
paperback publication 215, 219
past tense 27–8, 29
pen and paper writing 3, 7, 8
performance rights 216
personality of character
central character 63–4, 68, 70, 73–4, 76–81, 102–3
conveying information 34
dialogue purpose 170
plot 120–1
point of view 20, 26–7
subsidiary characters 92, 102, 103
phones 3, 4, 7, 8, 44, 51
photographs
central character 65, 82
physical locations 40–2
research 40–2, 46–8, 52, 53
subsidiary characters 105
physical appearance of character
central character 64–5, 67–9, 82–3
conveying information 34
first impressions 64–5, 67–9
point of view 20
subsidiary characters 105
unusual appearance 69
physical attractiveness of character 67, 82, 101
physical location 38–42, 52, 84, 146
pitching 194
place 38–42, 146, 146
place to write 2–3, 11–12
plot 109–42
act one: the beginning 119–26
act two: the middle 126–36
act three: the end 136–40
dialogue purpose 171
dramatic world 110–14
first chapters and prologues 115–19
managing characters 106
overview 109, 140–2
three-act structure 114–15
point of view (POV)
carrying dialogue 186, 187
central characters 62–3
first-person POV 21–3, 24, 35
first-person POV, third-person POV or omniscient 21–5
guidelines 25–7
mixing tenses and POVs 29
omniscient narration 18, 21, 24–5, 35
overview 18–19, 35
researching location 39
scenes 144, 151–5, 156, 165, 166
second-person POV 22
single POV or multiple POVs 19–21
subsidiary characters 106
telling the scene 151–5
telling the story 62–3
tenses 28–9
third-person POV 21–2, 23–4, 35

police 49, 55, 85, 110
practicalities of research 52–3
pre-emptive offers 213–14
present tense 27, 28–9
printing 217
print rights 215
productivity 2, 4
productivity apps 8
profession of character 72–3
progress tracking 2
prologues 22, 115–19
proofs 217
protecting work 7
psychological thrillers 20, 28
publication 215, 217, 219
publicity 216, 217–18
publishers
  finding a publisher 212–14
  identifying an agent 194, 195, 196
  managing relationship with 216–18
  negotiating a book deal 214–16
  translation rights 218–19
Publishers Weekly 213
publishing rights 213, 214, 215–16, 218–19
purpose
  of dialogue 169–73
  of scenes 145–50, 164

quantity and quality of writing 5
questions for reader 165

race of character 69
radio rights 219
reader engagement
  central character 63, 71, 84–5
  first chapters and prologues 116, 117, 118, 119
  research 39, 54–5
  scenes 144, 164–5, 166
  subsidiary characters 90
reader reports 192–3
reading aloud 192
reading fees 220
real events 56
re-enactment groups 50, 51
rejections 191, 194, 198
relationships
  dialogue 170, 171, 176–7, 183
  plot 111–12, 131–2
  subsidiary characters 100–2
  see also romantic relationships
religion of character 44, 45, 76, 103, 106, 112
reputation of agent 195
research 37–59
  accuracy 56
  context 42–8
  handling research 53–6
  identifying an agent 194
  inside knowledge 48–51
  managing characters 105
  natural world 51–2
  overview 37–8, 56–9
  physical locations 38–42
  practicalities 52–3
  and story 54–6
  what to research 38–53
resources 225–33
  editing software 231–3
  example synopsis 225–7
  software for writers 228–33
  writing software 228–31
response time from agent 197
resubmission 191, 197
revelations 71, 83, 97, 138, 160
rewriting 5–6, 191, 197, 212, 216, 217
rights 213, 214, 215–16, 218–19

risk 92, 134, 156, 158–9
rivalry of characters 74, 91, 112, 148–9
romance novels
  central character 61, 67, 82, 85
  choosing a theme 17–18
  dialogue purpose 169
  plot 135, 137
  scenes purpose 146–9
  subsidiary characters 89, 97
romantic relationships 40, 100–2, 131–2, 146–9, 157
royalties 211, 219

sales of book 214–15, 218, 219
sample chapters 198, 209–10, 221
sample covers 217
satellite imagery 42
saving work 7
scenes 143–67
  chapters and scenes 143–5
  conflict, risk, obstacles and subtext 156–62
  dialogue and control 176
  how to end 164–6
  how to start 155–6
  important moments 32
  overview 143, 167
  purpose 145–50
  when to end 164
  where to start 150–1
  who is in control 162–4
  who is telling the scene 151–5
schedules for writing 1, 2, 4
science fiction 118, 119
screens 10
seasons 51
second-person POV (point of view) 22
secrets 80–1, 94, 121, 160, 161
senses 39
sensitive information 49
sentences 31–2
setting 38–42, 84, 93, 118, 145–7
sex and gender 43–5, 63, 66, 206–7
shared central characters 61–2
showing and telling 34, 35, 76, 118
significant events 135–6, 172
single POV (point of view) 19–21, 35, 62–3
single-scene chapters 144
smartphones 4, 7, 8
social media 195, 199
Society of Authors 210, 216
software
  dictation 3
  editing software 231–3
  making use of technology 7–8
  software for writers 228–33
  writing software 228–31
speech 68, 105–6, 182–3, 187
spelling 8, 199, 217
spy stories 82, 137
start of novel *see* act one: the beginning
state of mind of character 73
story
  driving the story 62, 134–5
  ideas 8
  and research 54–6
  sample chapters 210
  telling the story 62–3
structural editing 216–17
style consistency 217
sub-agents 218
submissions
  checking the novel is finished 191
  covering letter 198–200

identifying an agent 193–8
overview 220–1
preparing the novel for submission 211
sample chapters 209–10
submitting to an agent 198–210
synopsis 200–9
sub-plots 78–9, 93, 104, 110–11, 116, 139
subsidiary characters 89–107
attraction to other characters 100–1
conflict for central character 102–4
hidden link to central character 98
hidden link to objective 97–8
influences on character 96–7
logical behaviour 99–100
managing characters 104–6
objective and motivation 95–6
overview 89, 107
relationships with other characters 101–2
truth telling 98–9
who they appear to be 94
who they are 94–104
why this particular character 89–94
subtext 156, 160–2
surprises 71, 80–1, 83, 94, 137–8, 160
synopsis 198, 200–9, 221, 225–7

targets for writing 2, 8, 11
technology 7–8, 51
television rights 213, 214, 216, 219
telling and showing 34, 35, 76, 118
tenses 27–9
tension
dialogue 187
plot objectives 124
point of view 20, 24
present tense 28
scenes 151, 154, 156, 161
subsidiary characters 92
themes 17–18, 77
third-person POV (point of view) 21–2, 23–4, 35
three-act structure
act one: the beginning 119–26
act two: the middle 126–36
act three: the end 136–40
and alternatives 139–40
first chapters and prologues 115–19
overview 114–15, 140–2
synopsis 208
thrillers 20, 28, 39, 137, 151
timeline of story 105, 116, 117, 120
time management 1, 11
title of book 217
tracking progress 2
translation rights 213, 214, 218, 219
travel writing 41, 46
trigger events 135–6
trust 9, 38
truth telling 98–9
twists 71, 81, 137–8, 160
Twitter 195, 199

UK and Commonwealth rights 215, 218, 219
unsolicited manuscripts 211

verbs 184–5
virtual worlds 114
virtues of character 77–8, 101
vocabulary 31, 182–3
voice of character 105–6, 182–3

walking, for health 10–11
war stories 44, 46–7, 93, 115, 118–19, 122–4, 129–30
weakness of character 129
weapons research 50
weather 38, 51
withholding information 82, 99, 121, 156, 166
word counts 2, 208–9
word processing packages 2, 8
words
  dialogue 182–3, 184–8
  and sentences 31–2
world-building 116, 146
world rights 214, 215, 218, 219
Writers & Artists 10, 193, 194
writers' groups 9, 192
writing competitions 200
writing courses 10, 211
writing longhand 3, 7, 8
writing novels *see* novel writing
writing organisations 194
writing practice 12–13
writing scenes *see* scenes
writing software 7–8, 228–31

YouTube 50